SAVED
from
THE SEA

hoo'

SAVED
from
THE SEA

Tales from Sea Life Centres

MARK OAKLEY

Whittet Books

TITLE PAGE ILLUSTRATION: Rocky watches excitedly as Missie and Silver are released into a special holding pen.

First published 1995
Text © 1995 Mark Oakley
Whittet Books Ltd, 18 Anley Road, London W14 OBY
Design by John Saunders

1 873580 19 3

British Library Cataloguing in Publication Data. A catalogue record for this book is available from the British Library.

The photographs are from Sea Life Centres except those listed on the following pages; for these, publishers and author are grateful to the following: Care for the Wild, 2/3, 10/11, 18, 20; Dr Ann Chase, 93; Exploris, 73; Julie Gachet, 92; Mark Stevens, 31, 33; Peter Richardson, 67, 69; Mark Stevens/British Divers Marine Life Rescue, 30, 31, 36; Bill Wilkinson, 45; Barry Williams, 22 (2), 23, 48, 49, 51, 55 (2), 56 (2), 57

Sea Life Centres are at the following addresses:

Oban Sea Life Centre, Barcaldine, Connel, Argyll tel 0631 72386
Weymouth Sea Life Park, Lodmoor Country Park, Weymouth, Dorset tel 0305 761070
Portsmouth Sea Life Centre, Clarence Esplanade, Southsea, Hants tel 0705 734461
St Andrews Sea Life Centre, The Scores, St Andrews, Fife tel 0334 474786
Hastings Sea Life Centre, Rock-a-Nore Rd, Hastings, East Sussex tel 0424 718776
Blackpool Sea Life Centre, Promenade, Blackpool, Lancs tel 0253 22445
Brighton Sea Life Centre, Marine Parade, Brighton, Sussex tel 0273 604234
Scarborough Sea Life Centre, Scalby Mills, Scarborough, N. Yorks tel 0723 376125
Rhyl Sea Life Centre, East Parade, Rhyl, Clwyd tel 0745 344660
Southend Sea Life Centre, Eastern Esplanade, Southend, Essex tel 0702 601834
Great Yarmouth Sea Life Centre, Marine Parade, Gt Yarmouth tel 0493330631
Hunstanton Sea Lfe Centre, Southern Promenade, Hunstanton, Norfolk tel 0485 533576
Tynemouth Sea Life Centre, Grand Parade, Tynemouth, Tyne and Wear tel 091 258 1031
Newquay Sea Life Centre, Towan Promenade, Newquay, Cornwall tel 0637 878134
Scheveningen Sea Life Centre, Strandweg 13, 2586 JK Den Haag, Scheveningen tel 010 31 70 3542100
Cornish Seal Sanctuary, Gweek, Nr Helston, Cornwall tel 0326 221361
Weston-Super-Mare Sea Life Centre, Marine Parade, Weston-Super-Mare tel 0934 641603
Blankenberge Sea Life Centre, Koning Albert 1, Laan 116, Blankenberge, Belgium tel 0032 50 42 42 00
Benalmadena Sea Life Centre, Puerto Marina, Benalmadena Costa, Spain

Printed and bound in Hong Kong by Wing King Tong

Contents

Author's Note   6

The Story of Missie and Silver   11

Spirit   21

Muddy   27

The Oban Seals   36

Sammy   48

Courtney and Duchess   53

Myrtle the Turtle   58

Goodbye Shirley and Valentine   64

Picasso   72

A Splint for a Sunfish!   79

Barney the Barnacle   84

The Amazing Weymouth Squirrel Fish!   87

By Royal Appointment   90

A Seal Called 'Handful'!   93

Author's Note

Not so long ago (fewer than four years ago in fact) I could have written all I knew about sea creatures on the shell of pea crab, and a pea crab — just to prove I have been paying attention these last few years — is smaller than a postage stamp!

On the subject of birds, on the other hand, I could warble on for hours, having been a keen bird-watcher since the age of nine and a licensed bird-ringer for nearly twenty years. My only experience with fish had been a two-year spell during which I made countless abortive expeditions to the banks of the Bridgewater Canal and drowned a few thousand maggots, usually to no purpose at all. In the entire period I caught only two fish, both of which must have had first to check very carefully that the bait was incapable of fighting back!

It simply never crossed my mind that life in our seas and oceans might be just as fascinating as bird life, and I would certainly have laughed at any suggestion that one day I might actually welcome the invitation to write a book on the subject.

Not that this collection of stories is in any sense an academic work. Rather it is a journalistic account of events surrounding some of the diverse sea creatures which have helped make my recent professional life a voyage of constant surprise and more than occasional delight. A voyage which has now completely stripped away those blinkers that once obscured my view of any wildlife other than that which bore feathers.

It began for me with an invitation to handle public relations for a new Sea Life Centre opening in 1990 on the famous Golden Mile in Blackpool, an assignment I enjoyed so much that later that same year I applied for and secured a full-time post with the Dorset-based company that operated that Centre, as well as another five similar attractions around the UK coast.

The oldest of these is the Oban Sea Life Centre on the shore of picturesque Loch Creran, which opened in 1979, the fruition of a scheme hatched years earlier by Scottish fish farmer, John Mace. Public interest in fish hatcheries had so flourished in the 1960s and early '70s that John became convinced there would be equal if not greater interest in a new style of aquarium displaying strictly native British marine creatures, rather than the colourful tropical varieties featured in traditional aquariums.

Sadly he died just months before the Oban Centre finally opened its doors under the stewardship of his son, David, with another son, Guy, providing keen support and assistance. He had lived long enough to see his dream taking shape, but would undoubtedly have taken great pleasure in the amazed and enthralled expressions of the first few visitors who trundled down the gravel track to view this curious new facility on the day of its unveiling.

The fish on display were of much the same variety to be found on any fishmonger's slab, but contained for the first time in surrounds which mimicked their natural habitats, providing them with ample freedom of movement behind viewing windows much larger and with much less obstructive frameworks than had ever previously been achieved anywhere within the British Isles.

A stunning centrepiece, which looks just as remarkable today, was the herring ring, a unique doughnut-shaped tank in which a shoal of silvery herring swam in continuous circuit, watched either from the outside or from a special observation platform at the centre. Many visitors were astounded to discover that the seas around our own coasts host several species of sharks, and to be able to watch some of those species gliding silently by just inches in front of their faces.

The Sea Life Centre opened a window onto the fascinating world beneath the waves, and word quickly spread of the many delights and surprises to be sampled there. Within twelve months, it had become the leading visitor attraction on the Scottish West Coast, and when outdoor pools and rescue facilities for sick, injured and abandoned seal pups were added at a later stage, they boosted its appeal still further.

Today there are well over a dozen Sea Life Centres around the UK coastline, another at the Dutch seaside resort of Scheveningen and more opening every year.

In February 1993 the popular Cornish Seal Sanctuary, a rescue and rehabilitation centre for Grey Seal pups since 1957, became another valuable branch of this steadily blossoming network which now introduces more than four million people every year to the beauty and complexity of our native marine environment. It can be a startling revelation.

A qualified marine biologist, David Mace, encouraged other

marine experts to join him. Many are still with the company today and their ranks have been considerably swelled since those first few years at Oban. Each possesses an infectious enthusiasm for his or her subject, coupled with a genuine affection for the creatures in their care, whose welfare they would never allow to be compromised in the interests of mere commerce.

A recipe for conflict? Happily, not in this case, for the whole ethos of Sea Life Centres hinges on the presentation of marine life in as near natural a setting as possible, and probably the most significant difference for the creatures themselves is that their artificial environment is inevitably a whole lot cleaner and healthier than the real thing. Displays are free of pollution, generally very spacious, carefully themed and their inhabitants — free of the gauntlet of natural hazards faced by their wild counterparts — frequently live much longer and healthier lives. The idea is to stimulate an appreciation of the true value of our seas and the desirability of safeguarding their future.

Though never actually scribed onto tablets of stone, the Sea Life Centre policy in respect of which creatures were to be displayed and which not was a very simple one. In essence, any British sea creature, bar mammals, that settled into a display without any apparent stress or other ill effects, was considered suitable for inclusion. The more comprehensive the collection, the better the impression visitors would receive of the richness and diversity of our native marine environment.

Seals are now featured at some Centres solely as a result of rescue programmes, and in the majority of cases they are released once fully fit and able to fend for themselves. Tropical sharks are displayed at only two Centres, where it was possible to construct displays large enough to accommodate them with the same freedom of movement and quality of care afforded to every other resident sea creature, and where strenuous efforts are made to convey a powerful conservation message on behalf of sharks the world over. So many of the world's larger sharks are under serious threat from both commercial and sports fishing that this rare exception to the 'strictly native' policy was considered amply justified. The image of sharks held by youngsters who witness these displays, read the accompanying information panels and listen to educational 'shark talks' is vastly different from that held by many people who were influenced by the *Jaws* phenomenon.

A similar environmental message in relation to all the resident creatures is reinforced through a wealth of environmentally angled interpretation, and the experience made more personal through a host of interactive opportunities — like the chance to handle sturdy rock-pool creatures such as crabs and starfish, or hand-feed an inquisitive and often greedy thornback ray.

What impressed me more than all this, however, and provided the inspiration for this book was the way the Sea Life Centres and the Seal Sanctuary often interact themselves, in a very positive manner, with the real marine environment.

Soon after my arrival a new conservation scheme called SeaWatch was launched, in part to provide our visitors with the opportunity to take a more personal role in marine conservation, but also to nourish and nurture that interactive aspect, providing the means and the expertise to time and again play a very direct role in helping sea creatures of all kinds. A subscription scheme, SeaWatch provides generous benefits to its supporters and channels the funds received into a variety of conservation endeavours.

In 1994, for example, SeaWatch provided a £2,500 boost to a Whale and Dolphin Conservation Society research project studying the dolphins around the Cornish coast; a £3,500 grant to a researcher investigating the lives of, and hazards faced by Cornish cave-dwelling Grey Seals and £2,000 for the Isle of Man Basking Shark project, as well as helping the Sea Life Centres themselves to fund often costly marine life rescue missions.

The stories that follow serve as testament to the success of that endeavour. All concern creatures which for diverse reasons have created media headlines during the three eventful years of my employment with Sea Life, though some of their stories began much earlier.

In most cases, of course, I have no reliable reference source about their circumstances before they came into the caring hands of one or other of my numerous widespread colleagues, and similarly there is seldom irrefutable evidence regarding the subsequent fortunes of those that eventually went their own way again.

I hope you will therefore indulge a certain degree of informed conjecture and journalistic licence. After all, my guesswork, as I am sure you will agree, is seldom more unlikely or amazing than the known facts.

The Story of Missie and Silver

It was a typically bleak winter's day in December 1990 when I first met Missie and Silver. A biting sea breeze penetrated bone deep in the short time it took to walk from the car to the curious chapel-like building on Marine Drive which housed the offices of the Brighton Aquarium. My new employers were about to acquire the lease of this historic attraction, and I was there simply to take a look round and learn as much as I could before the impending take-over. My guide led me into a rickety lift and we descended noisily to the Aquarium itself, the journey giving the impression of a plummet into some dark subterranean cavern, instead of merely to a level with the surface of the nearby English Channel. As the lift door was thrown back the illusion was enhanced rather than diminished, our footsteps echoing eerily on the hard stone floor as we emerged into a long and dimly lit arched arcade.

I remember very little of what passed during the next twenty or thirty minutes, beyond the fact that I was invited to peer through a succession of rectangular windows at a variety of exotic tropical fish, and that somewhere en route I was also introduced to a crocodile and a pair of sea-lions. One of those sea-lions — a huge male called Rocky — is now enjoying retirement at the Cornish Seal Sanctuary, and the crocodile went to an unusual new animal reserve in the Canary Islands ... but those are other stories. This tale concerns the two animals I visited next on my tour, and this bit I remember very well indeed.

We arrived eventually at a dismal cafeteria, with a long single line of tables all hugging a gently curving whitewashed wall into which were built a series of windows. As we drew level with the first of

Silver is still very trusting of humans after several weeks in the pasture, approaching to within a few feet of an underwater cameraman.

those windows, a sleek and smiling face suddenly appeared on its opposite side.

'That's Missie,' said my guide. 'She's a lot smaller than Silver.' As if responding to cue, the larger male dolphin appeared gliding gracefully by in the background.

We made our way via a series of passageways and steps to the dolphinarium itself, a roughly circular auditorium with the surface of the dolphin pool at the centre, like the bottom of a polished bowl. This had been home to Missie and Silver for a combined total of 33 years, during which time they had thrilled countless thousands of holidaymakers with a regular routine designed to show off their natural agility as well as their apparent intelligence.

Silver was the younger of the two, having spent just 12 years at the Aquarium compared to Missie's 21 years. Missie had in fact spent most of her life there. She was reportedly just 6 months old when fished from the wild in the basin of the Mississippi, from which she got her name.

By the time I met Missie and Silver and watched entranced as they circled their pool chattering to each other with a series of clicks and whistles, controversy had been raging for years over the morality of keeping dolphins and other cetaceans captive to provide entertainment for humans. The debate had recently scaled new heights with the emergence of an ambitious scheme involving a large male Bottle-nosed Dolphin called Rocky, who, after years of performing at an outdoor dolphinarium in Morecambe, was destined to become one of the first ever captive dolphins to regain his liberty.

A generous conch, or sea snail, farmer with an eighty-acre lagoon on Providenciales in the remote and idyllic Turks and Caicos islands had been persuaded by disillusioned former dolphin trainer Doug Cartlidge to fence off the lagoon from the open ocean to serve as a rehabilitation facility, where Rocky might gradually re-acquire all the natural instincts and skills necessary for his survival in the wild, prior to his release into the open ocean. Doug eventually managed to mobilize an international coalition of animal charities behind the project, steered in the UK by Zoo Check and funded by a major appeal launched by the *Mail on Sunday*.

The scheme was not without its opponents, not least among the few remaining wildlife attraction operators in Europe with captive dolphins of their own, and indeed, when the time came for Rocky to begin his journey, an ugly confrontation between the rival factions led to the operation being postponed. It needed court action to resolve the situation, but finally in mid-January 1991 Rocky was flown out to his new Caribbean island paradise.

The flight lasted something like nine hours, and it was an anxious time for all involved. Suspended in a canvas sling and smoth-

Rocky (centre), Missie (left) and Silver in their 80-acre pasture.

ered from beak to tail in cold cream to prevent his delicate skin drying out, Rocky's condition was carefully monitored by Richard Kock, curator and veterinary officer of Whipsnade Wild Animal Park.

Several hours into the journey, with all apparently going well, Richard decided to try and grab a couple of hours of long overdue sleep ... only to be woken within half an hour by worried helpers alarmed at a sudden dramatic increase in Rocky's respiration rate. Dolphins, unlike humans, do not breathe automatically. The acts of exhalation and inhalation require a conscious decision on their part, and consequently the frequency of breathing is considered a good indicator of a dolphin's mental condition. Discomfort or distress tend to stimulate a more rapid breathing sequence. So, it would seem, can at least one other form of stimulant!

It was not until a series of emergency tests had drawn puzzling blanks that Richard's attention was transferred to a pretty air stewardess, who was affectionately tickling Rocky's chin and talking to him in what she no doubt considered were suitably soothing tones. Rather than being soothed, however, Rocky's reaction was altogether more typical of most mature, warm blooded males in similar circumstances, and Richard was not at all surprised to see his breathing resume a more normal, relaxed pattern once the stewardess had been persuaded to make herself scarce.

Within a few days of his triumphant arrival at American Chuck

Hesse's conch farm, Rocky seemed to be happily exploring the full expanse of his new eighty-acre domain; also within days, the decision had been made to provide him with two companions, namely Brighton dolphins Missie and Silver.

Sea Life had completed their negotiations to take over the Brighton Aquarium, and the company's own marine experts had carried out an exhaustive investigation among cetacean authorities world-wide before concluding that the best option for Missie and Silver was to follow in Rocky's wake.

Retaining their services as entertainers had never been an option. None of the Sea Life Centres keeps performing animals of any kind, besides which my colleagues simply felt that after so many years Missie and Silver had earned at least the chance of retirement and the opportunity once more to enjoy the freedom of the open seas. The apparent success of the Rocky mission provided all the encouragement necessary to plan and prepare for the subsequent transport of the Brighton pair, a process involving a comprehensive series of veterinary checks and negotiations to find an airline willing to take on board so unusual a cargo.

At one stage it appeared that Missie might be pregnant, a condition which would certainly have ruled out her movement and — in the event of a tiny bundle arriving — would have further complicated matters since it would have been unlikely that a new youngster could safely have made such a marathon trip and equally inconceivable to separate mother and baby.

There were other reasons why a pregnant Missie would not have been a happy circumstance. Two previous offspring had both died at very tender ages, leading to speculation that Missie and Silver — originating from different parts of the world — were genetically mismatched, and unlikely to ever produce a completely healthy infant. Test results thankfully confirmed that we were dealing with a phantom, and the stalled air-lift plans were back on the runway.

All went like clockwork until the night of March 18th, the eve of their departure from Gatwick, when Missie and Silver watched warily as a team of volunteers from the British Divers Marine Life Rescue organization struggled into their diving suits at the side of the pool. The plan was simple. The two dolphins would be herded in turn into a smaller holding pen adjacent to the main pool, then each lifted from the water in nets to be transferred into the carefully designed open-top containers which were to support them until they reached the Caribbean. No-one was under any illusion that Missie and Silver were going to enjoy this first stage of the operation, but neither did anyone suspect just how difficult it would turn out to be.

Silver gave himself up with scarcely even a token struggle, but

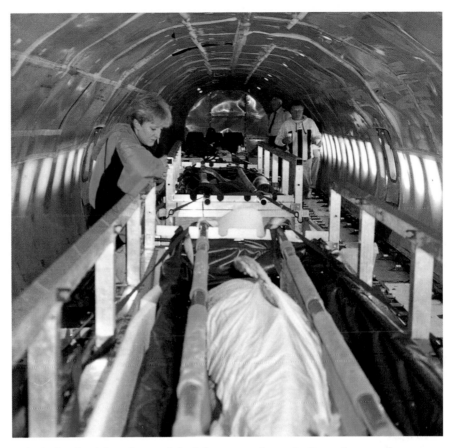

All aboard and ready for take-off.

Missie had evidently rumbled the game long before she saw her part-ner unceremoniously hoisted from the water, and she proceeded to frustrate her would-be captors by continuously dodging between them, even leaping straight over the top of their net when they spread this in an effort to cut off her escape route.

As time dragged by it became clear that Missie was starting to enjoy this novel new pastime, but the divers — some of them now half drowned — were getting seriously worried. Silver was settled in his container, already liberally smothered in cream and buoyed by a reservoir of salt water to give him extra support and keep him cool.

By this time a posse of photographers and TV crews had already positioned themselves on the apron at Gatwick airport, ready to record Missie and Silver's departure, completely oblivious to the fact that the said departure was currently being seriously jeopardized by a mischievous Missie. In the end one of the divers resorted to rugby tactics, executing a perfect water-borne flying tackle to hang on grimly to the thrashing Missie while his colleagues came to his aid. Her fun over, Missie was whisked from the water and deposited in the second container where Richard Kock treated her to the same moisturizing body rub already applied to Silver.

A combination of ramps, hoists and brute strength saw both containers quickly transferred to a waiting lorry and the first leg of the journey was underway. I was with the waiting press already at Gatwick, stamping each foot alternately on the tarmac to revive freezing toes and watching the sky gradually brighten from the east, wondering if all was going according to plan. Inevitably my mind drifted back to that first introduction to Missie and Silver. I recalled my horror at realizing that the only daylight either had seen for twelve years was the little which filtered through a short length of frosted skylight set high up in one corner … down below knee-height for anyone walking the footpath up on Marine Drive.

Over in the east an orange cast to the horizon indicated that the sun would soon be up.

'Another half-hour and Missie and Silver will be needing dark glasses,' I thought to myself. It wasn't quite that long, though, before an airport luggage transporter rounded a bend in the distance, and we could make out the two large containers housing the two dolphins, with people standing on either side waving to the waiting reception committee. Grant Stenhouse, manager of Brighton Sea Life Centre, jumped from the slow moving trailer and walked towards me, his beaming smile immediately assuring me that everything was in order. He quickly told me about the fun and games with Missie, but was much more excited about the conversation the two dolphins had apparently been having with each other all the way from the coast.

'They've been clicking away at each other non-stop,' said Grant. 'It's like each is making sure the other is still close by, and it seems to have helped them stay calm.'

The clicking carried on as the containers were transferred to a waiting hydraulic lift which slowly raised them to a level with the aircraft's cargo doors. A concerted heave saw both safely into the cargo hold, then those of us not privileged enough to be making the journey with them retreated to a safe distance as the aircraft began taxi-ing to the runway. Minutes later we saw the 707 powering skywards, and most of us watched until the aircraft was no more than a distant speck.

We were an emotional little group, but there were two amongst us who were undoubtedly even more moved than the rest by the morning's events. They had stood by quietly as the dolphins were boarded, and, apart from obliging the media with brief interviews, had scarcely spoken at all. Their faces, though, were open books, and they read of the realization of long harboured dreams, of cherished hopes and firm convictions about the essential 'rightness' of what was taking place. They might perhaps have been thinking of a curious similarity in the plot of this still unfolding story and another, older story about orphaned lion cubs. They were, of course, Zoo Check's founders, Bill Travers and Virginia McKenna.

Nine and a half hours later in the Turks and Caicos islands, there was a similar expression on the face of Lee Chanona, the man designated to supervise the rehabilitation of Rocky, Missie and Silver. It had been a long time, but Lee knew Missie and Silver well. He had once been their trainer at Brighton. Their chattering increased when he greeted the pair, suggesting recognition of a familiar and trusted voice.

After a bumpy ride from the small island airport Missie and Silver were lowered into a special medical pen, shielded from the bright sunshine by a bamboo canopy, essential protection for skin which hadn't felt the sun's ultra-violet rays for so long. Immediately Rocky raced across the lagoon to see the new arrivals. He stayed at the side of the pen for hours, following Missie and Silver as they circuited the pen's interior, sometimes just resting his head on the bars and watching.

All the numerous helpers who assisted Missie and Silver's delivery into their temporary pen were astounded at how fit and well both appeared to be, after such a lengthy trip. After five days a full veterinary examination took place and blood samples were taken. Two days later, on March 27th, they were given a clean bill of health and released into the lagoon, instantly setting off to explore this strange new environment. Curiously Rocky kept his distance. Perhaps he sensed a strong bond between the newcomers and feared Silver might resent the close proximity of a rival male. Maybe he wanted to allow them time to find their own bearings, or maybe he was simply being shy.

The report that landed on my desk the morning after March 28th brightened my whole day, and that of every colleague I showed it too. It read:

'Silver and Missie have been bow-riding after only two days in the pasture. Bow-riding is a wild-learned behaviour, something Missie certainly hasn't done for 21 years. Whether it is memory or something they have just learned, it is incredible.

'Both dolphins are looking so well, so lively and already so independent. If anyone here retained any doubts, they have now been banished forever.'

The bulletins got better and better. The report for the 29th described Rocky's decision finally to join the other two, his presence accepted without incident and prompting the comment: 'To look at the three of them, you would think that they were wild dolphins!'

On April 5th Lee Chanona began the process of introducing live fish to them. Missie caught one, tossed it up and swallowed it. 'We all breathed a sigh of relief,' noted my informant. On April 13th a sociable wild dolphin christened Jojo appeared at the pasture fence and spent the whole afternoon there.

'Rocky, Silver and Missie weren't at all disturbed by his presence, and all four dolphins were whistling and clicking (chatting) away quite happily.'

Another slight worry was dispelled on April 17th when Silver finally emulated Missie's example and scooped up a live fish.

'Their progress is faster than we had ever expected and they are already well on their way to being fully rehabilitated.'

The project's opponents dismissed all such news as propaganda, and whilst it was difficult to conceive of a credible motive for such deceit, I was nevertheless worried that perhaps the reports were coloured by an overwhelming desire for a successful outcome. Those niggling worries vanished in August, when fifteen-year-old Caroline Lane, from East Molesey in Surrey, took a trip to the Turks and Caicos Islands as first prize-winner in a competition set up by Sea Life with a national children's publication. Caroline's first-hand report following her trip could not have been more conclusive. Of her first sight of Missie and Silver since a visit to Brighton as a toddler, Caroline wrote:

'I cannot describe how fantastic it was seeing them in the wild and being so close to the dolphins. They were so relaxed in their new home, and it was good to see how unrestricted they were in their eighty-acre lagoon.'

She added that all three dolphins had been declared fit for release into the open ocean, and in mid-September the long-awaited moment arrived. To prevent their heading straight for popular holiday

Missie and Silver are greeted by their new companion Rocky.

beaches around Providenciales they were released several miles away close to the coast of a neighbouring island, and within days had been reported sighted in the company of other wild dolphins.

It must have been hard for Lee Chanona and the project team to turn their boats around and effectively abandon Rocky, Missie and Silver, leaving them finally to determine their own fates. Opponents renounced the move as cruel, and it wasn't long before a photograph appeared in a Brighton paper allegedly captured by an underwater cameraman and purporting to show an emaciated and starving Silver.

Strange though, in light of this photographer's claims to have swum in Silver's company for quite a length of time, that he had failed to photograph his dorsal fin, which would have established his identity beyond doubt. A cynic like myself might point out that someone had omitted to inform the 'opposition' that Missie and Silver had been painlessly but quite clearly freeze-branded with the symbols for female and male, precisely to facilitate future identification. And in contrast with this alleged sighting, those symbols were prominently highlighted in a flurry of sightings almost two years later, from islanders and holidaymakers on Providenciales. You can imagine the delight those sightings prompted among Sea Life staff and all the various charity volunteers who had been involved.

There's no cast-iron proof as yet that Missie, Silver and Rocky are still alive and flourishing somewhere out there in the wild blue

The three dolphins are soon happily swimming together ... often at high speed.

yonder. Perhaps that in itself is the most positive sign we could hope for. After all, wouldn't the instinctive reaction of three formerly captive dolphins who found they couldn't cope with freedom be to head towards the nearest human-inhabited coastline? I have no doubt we would have heard about it had that been the case. But any debate over their competence — or lack of such — for a renewed life of liberty misses the point as far as I am concerned.

The point is that they deserved the chance to give it their best shot. After a month or two in their lagoon pasture they were no longer the same animals that they had been in Brighton and Morecambe. The change had been particularly noticeable in Missie and Silver, their skin almost visibly losing the sores acquired through years of exposure to water-cleansing chemicals, and their dull lifeless eyes regaining that glint so noticeable in truly wild dolphins. Had they at this time been able to choose for themselves between a return to concrete pools in Britain and the call of the wild there is no doubt in my mind which course they would have chosen.

Missie and Silver waste no time in exploring every corner of their new temporary home.

Spirit

Perhaps more so than any other creatures on earth, whales and dolphins seem capable of inciting extraordinary human endeavour on their behalf.

Man has always had an affinity with dolphins; stories abound of dolphins saving people from drowning and also trying to rescue their own kind. Dolphins are now recognized as having a high intelligence; so to most of us the heavy toll of dolphins killed or trapped accidentally in nets is a cause of great regret. There are of course still some nations and peoples to whom whales and dolphins represent no more than a valuable but increasingly rare commodity.

So while high-speed whaling ships equipped with rocket-propelled harpoons still reap carnage among herds of grazing whales in some parts of the world, conservationists will mobilize dramatic resources to save the lives of just two gray whales trapped by an advancing ice flow in Alaska; and hundreds of thousands of people in Britain will dig deep in their pockets to help send three dolphins to freedom in the Caribbean.

And when a solitary exhausted dolphin is washed up on a sandy beach in Cornwall, the ensuing rescue mission inspires no less urgency or commitment than would a similar mission to save a human life. Exactly how this dolphin, later named Spirit, came to be in such a situation will probably never be firmly established. He was discovered at Gwithian, Cornwall, on August 22nd, 1992; he was a Common Dolphin, a species which — as the name suggests — is one of the most numerous in the world's seas and oceans. By rights he should have been far out at sea in the company of many others of his kind, and his predicament suggested he was either badly injured or suffering a serious illness.

Some scientists contend that whales and dolphins use the earth's

Even minor wounds like these on Spirit's beak can bleed profusely in dolphins, because of the efficiency with which their powerful hearts pump blood around their bodies.

invisible magnetic contours as a navigational aid when finding their way around the oceans. When a group of whales and dolphins accustomed to deep water ventures too close to shore it can risk getting stranded on gently sloping shorelines where echolocation fails to signal any prominent obstacle. Thus species that normally live close to land, like the Harbour Porpoise and Bottle-nosed Dolphin, for example, are almost never involved in 'mass strandings', being too familiar with the shape of the coastline to make such a mistake. When individuals of those species are found high and dry, say the experts, that is almost certainly a symptom of an individual's problem. In other words they have floated ashore because they are dying.

There is a long list of failed rescue attempts involving mature Harbour Porpoises which tends to support this theory, and it is not

Some of the cuts and scrapes collected by Spirit during his stranding are clearly visible on his flanks and dorsal fin.

Concern is etched on the face of Sanctuary worker Sally Tomkins as she joins other helpers keeping Spirit afloat.

difficult to conceive that the action of currents and tides could eventually bring ashore a dolphin that began to fall sick far beyond land.

Happily for Spirit, it seems there was nothing wrong with him until he unwittingly and mysteriously found himself in the unfamiliar territory of shallow waters off the Gwithian shoreline. Maybe he had lost both his bearings and his fellow dolphins in stormy seas, though the weather prior to his discovery was fairly mild, so a more likely explanation is that he had been snared for a while in fishing nets. Whatever brought him there in the first place, it was undoubtedly the gentle gradient of the beach that led him to get stranded, and the panic and stress afterwards that left him so exhausted.

Once discovered, he was hastily transported across Cornwall to the Cornish Seal Sanctuary at Gweek, where resident veterinary surgeon, James Barnett, immediately instigated a desperate rescue programme which was to last thirteen days.

Luckily most of the seal pups rescued by the Sanctuary over the previous winter had already gone back to the wild, and only a few stragglers needed to be transferred from a small isolation pool to make room for Spirit. When he first arrived, though, Spirit was too weak to keep himself afloat, and had to be aided by Sanctuary staff and other willing volunteers. He was gently walked around the pool to try and stimulate him to swim independently and thus take the first vital step on the long road to recovery. It was not until late afternoon of the following day, however, that Spirit finally responded and began swimming under his own steam. James Barnett had taken swabs and samples from Spirit on his arrival, and when the results came back the news was good. No signs of any serious ailments or infections: nothing to suggest that Spirit shouldn't make a full recovery.

During his first seven days at the Sanctuary Spirit was never alone. Two-person teams worked two-hour shifts to keep him under constant observation, often spending time in the pool with him. He seemed to enjoy company and his respiratory rate often slowed when he was joined in the water. By the sixth day his strength was quite clearly returning. All he now needed was sufficient time to recover completely from his ordeal.

A further week went by, punctuated by regular feeding sessions and plenty of exercise periods. Finally James reckoned he was well enough to resume life in the open sea, but his release was an operation that required very careful planning and the co-operation of a great many willing accomplices. These even included the British Waterbed Company, who sent mattresses on which to lie Spirit for his journey back to freedom, and a team of navy divers from RNAS Culdrose led by Chief Diving Officer Neil Primrose.

A team of eight Sanctuary staff first lifted Spirit from his pool in a makeshift stretcher, then lowered him onto the mattresses on the Sanctuary's own trailer. He was covered with towels and sheets, all soaked with sea water. The only part of his body left exposed was his blowhole, and the skin around this was smeared with lanolin to prevent it drying out. Four people then joined him in the trailer for the short journey to the boatyard, where the slipway had been cleared and both Spirit's boat and three other escorting vessels were ready waiting.

The Navy had provided two rigid-hull inflatables, across one of which they had constructed a platform for both dolphin and mattress. Just prior to the transfer from trailer to boat, however, James Barnett gave Spirit a final shot of long-lasting antibiotic. He was then carefully carried and laid in position and the tiny flotilla began its outbound voyage, turning south at the mouth of the river and scything through the waves for a full half-mile before engines were cut. The second inflatable lined up alongside the first and the two were held together to prevent a capsize as Spirit was then lowered over the side and into the water with a neatly executed half-roll on entry.

For several seconds everyone held their breaths as Spirit sank beneath the surface, but then his dorsal fin emerged … and he was away. No time spent taking bearings, nor even relishing the feel of being back in his own environment. Spirit just pointed his beak at the horizon and turned up the throttle.

Choppy conditions meant he was soon lost to sight from those watching from the boats, but the Seal Sanctuary's own 'eye-in-the-sky', an experienced cameraman aboard a navy Sea King helicopter, managed to follow his progress for a good four or five minutes as he accelerated away from the coast.

None of the Sanctuary staff who was privileged enough to be among the observers could find adequate words to describe their feelings at the moment of Spirit's speedy departure, and a kind of reverent silence descended on all the boats as they made their way back to harbour. Fortunately they have been able to re-live that special moment many times over, as have many thousands of Sanctuary visitors watching the whole event captured on film and relayed at regular intervals on a monitor in the seal hospital.

No-one had been more gratified, nor more relieved by Spirit's successful departure than vet, James Barnett, who had called upon all of his vast experience to hasten his unique patient's recovery. It was a personal triumph which boded well for any future stranded dolphins, and indeed within two weeks of Spirit's release a second dolphin casualty arrived at the Sanctuary.

The RSPCA telephoned on September 16th with news of an injured dolphin near Porthminster at St Ives. A team from the Sanctuary was soon on its way, equipped with air mattresses and water sprayers, but on arrival they learned that the dolphin had vanished. Two RSPCA officers had been supporting it in shallow water in a tiny cove, until the advancing tide threatened to block off their own escape route. Hoping for the best, they had waded out as deep as they dared with the dolphin between them, then given it a final push out to sea before retreating to dry land. They had watched as the dolphin swam slow circles before disappearing round the headland and out of view.

There was nothing for the Sanctuary crew to do but head back to Gweek, where the seals, sea-lions, penguins, donkeys and one sheep were bid goodnight and everyone departed for home. Shortly before midnight, however, a staff member raised the alert. The RSPCA had called again to say the dolphin had re-appeared on an open beach and was now definitely on its way to the Sanctuary. Half a dozen bleary-eyed staff began the arduous task of emptying the seal's isolation pool of both seals and water. The seals were not best pleased at being evicted to other smaller premises at such an unsociable hour, but then those charged with moving them were not too thrilled at the prospect either.

The pool was re-filled with clean water just in the nick of time. No sooner had the pumps been turned off than the RSPCA arrived, their vehicle towing what looked like a horse box, inside which the injured dolphin was suspended in a sling.

Unfortunately James Barnett was at this time in the Crimea checking the health of Brightness, the beluga whale, but local vet George Bates was quick to answer the latest dolphin distress call.

It needed only a glance at this latest casualty to deduce that he was in far worse shape than Spirit had been. He was covered from beak to tail in fine cuts and abrasions, and his beak itself appeared badly damaged. Nevertheless he was hastily transferred to the isolation pool where staff and volunteers began the familiar routine of walking him in circles. A diving club member, chatting quietly as he took his turn in the water, revealed that the dolphin had been christened 'Bang Bang', after a Chinese culinary delicacy which this same diver had been on his way out to sample when diverted by news of the dolphin's rescue.

Throughout the night and most of the next day Bang Bang clung to life by a slender thread, while an increasingly desperate battle was fought to improve his condition. Sadly, in spite of antibiotics, multivitamins, steroids … and the sheer force of will of every person present, Bang Bang died at 8pm on September 17th. A post mortem revealed that his upper and lower jaws were badly smashed, undoubtedly causing pain, stress and trauma from which he had been unable to recover. There were more than a few tears shed over Bang Bang's demise, the blow to morale perhaps all the heavier in light of the euphoria which followed the successful rescue of Spirit.

It was a sobering reminder that in most cases, the stranding of a single cetacean is likely to be just a symptom of a more serious problem, rather than the problem itself, and that often the casualty will already be too far gone for rescue. James Barnett is certainly only too well aware that for every 'Spirit' there are likely be two or three 'Bang Bangs' at least. He remained confident that there would be other successes, however, and he was to be proved right almost exactly one year later with a dolphin called Muddy …

Muddy

The Bottle-nosed Dolphin, Rocky, referred to in the earlier story about Missie and Silver, was probably the first real live dolphin I ever saw. I watched him perform at Morecambe Marineland on a family day out from Manchester when I was about eleven years old. Some ten years later I enjoyed a rare glimpse of porpoises in the Firth of Forth, but it was not until the summer of 1993 that I had the privilege of seeing my first wild dolphins.

I was on holiday with my wife and seven-year-old daughter at a villa on the Costa Del Sol. The balcony looked straight out onto the Mediterranean, and during that twilight period after a hard day's sunbathing, prior to heading off to town for the evening meal, I used to prop my elbows on the whitewashed balcony wall and stare out to sea through 10 x 50 binoculars, hoping to catch a glimpse of some avian delight such as a Cory's Shearwater, a graceful and fairly common sea-bird in these parts but a rarity around the coast of Britain.

On one particular evening, after claiming the shower ahead of the women and dressing hurriedly to ensure the longest possible session with my trusty binoculars, I was peering avidly at the distant crests and ripples of the breeze-caressed sea when something distinctly other than a sea-bird bobbed into view.

Light was failing fast, but there could be no mistaking those sleek silhouettes arcing up out of the water and back down again in rapid fluid motion. A school of some 30 to 40 dolphins was making its way steadily westwards towards the Atlantic.

Until that moment I hadn't even known dolphins ventured into the Mediterranean, but after that first thrilling sighting I was to spy two more schools before our holiday came to an end, plus a small school of more ponderous dark whales which I assumed to be pilot whales.

All the dolphins were much too distant for certain identification, but the most numerous species in the Mediterranean is the oceanic Striped Dolphin. The general shape certainly matched their description and it is more than likely that at least some of those I saw belonged to this species … which makes what I was to learn immediately on arrival back at work in Dorset all the more ironic. For what should be swimming around at the Sea Life Centre in Weymouth but a Striped Dolphin.

His name was Muddy, and when I arrived at Weymouth to take my first look at him, I was not in the least surprised to find him sharing his indoor pool with James Barnett. Gradually I was able to piece together what was a fairly dramatic tale, which had started about a week earlier.

James had been on his way back from Padstow harbour, where, together with a team of divers, he had been hoping to net a rogue adult male Grey Seal which had been enjoying a luxury diet at the expense of three highly disgruntled salmon fishermen. Each time they hauled in their nets in the lower reaches of the River Camel, this enterprising seal appeared from nowhere to help itself to some of the finer specimens. This had been going on for some while, and one of the three fishermen had lately threatened to dispose of the raider with a high-powered rifle. He would have been acting within the law had he carried out his threat, and so James and his helpers from the Southern and British Marine Life rescue organizations devised an alternative solution. The plan was to try and net the seal in the river at its shallowest point and then to move it across country to the south coast of Cornwall, well away from any salmon fishing, but at the eleventh hour the plan was changed when it was learned that the same seal had found an even richer source of food, namely the tourists in Padstow harbour.

This was great news for the seal pursuit team, or so they thought. Laying a trap across the mouth of the harbour was a far simpler operation than attempting to catch a solitary Grey Seal in the expansive Camel estuary. The problem was that somebody evidently tipped off the seal, which must have hauled itself out somewhere just up the coast and used its sharp eyesight to watch as the net was spread across the harbour and left there for twenty hours before James and the divers decided enough was enough, and packed up to head off home.

Their only consolation was the knowledge that the salmon season had just three more weeks to run, and that all the publicity surrounding the abortive capture attempt might prove sufficient to prevent that furious fisherman from employing more lethal tactics. It did!

Concern for the Camel seal had to take a back seat, however, when the call came through that a dolphin had stranded on mudflats at Christchurch, near Bournemouth. James and his companions had no hesitation in turning around and heading for Dorset.

The message had been a little vague over the dolphin's exact whereabouts, and after tramping the mudflats for half an hour or so they learned that he was being supported in the water on the opposite side of the harbour. Luckily, a boat arrived to ferry James and two others across. They were amazed to find the dolphin being kept afloat by a heavily pregnant woman, and even more amazed to learn that she had been nursing him for nearly two hours. Needless to say she was warmly thanked by those arriving to offer her relief at last, but it would have been nice to have arranged some special reward for her at a later stage. She departed without leaving either a name or an address, however, and all attempts to track her down came to nought. She may have chosen to remain anonymous to avoid the glare of publicity which would almost certainly have resulted from such a selfless and heroic deed.

The dolphin, for whom the name Muddy was an obvious and instant choice, given that he was found at Mudeford Quay, appeared to be suffering primarily from exhaustion. He was badly cut up, probably as a direct result of the stranding, and was noticeably underweight. James later suggested that he may have lost touch with his 'school-mates' possibly following bullying from other young males seeking to assert their dominance or perhaps even adults, and had then drifted gradually towards land, eventually finding himself in Christchurch harbour.

Unfortunately for Muddy his arrival there coincided with the staging of a sailing regatta, which activity no doubt added to his distress and led to his swimming further upstream into the network of channels making up the Christchurch mudflats.

James gave Muddy some emergency first aid while other helpers managed somehow to commandeer a van. There was no question of driving all the way back down to Cornwall though. Muddy was in no condition for such a marathon journey as that. But as luck would have it an alternative, and perhaps even better facility, was available just an hour's drive away at Weymouth.

Weymouth Sea Life Park houses an extensive fish quarantine and collection complex, dozens of circular pools of various sizes and depths where different species of sea creature are kept before being transferred either to other Sea Life Centres around the coast, or into the public aquarium displays at Weymouth itself. In the spring of 1993 work had begun on the installation of the biggest 'holding' pool yet: oval in shape and measuring 14 metres long by 9 wide, designed to house British sharks, perhaps even the semi-tropical blue sharks which occur annually off the south-west coast of Britain.

It was just sheer happy coincidence that the pool was finally

Muddy is subjected to a thorough medical examination by vet James Barnett.

completed at exactly the same time as Muddy's stranding. No filter bed or filter pumps had yet been installed, but James Barnett still felt the pool would be ideal for Muddy's convalescence. A phone call while he and fellow rescuers had been en route to Christchurch had alerted Weymouth's quarantine manager, Robin James, who had immediately started the pumps to fill the new pool to a depth of almost 1.5 metres. The last few gallons were still gushing forth as the van bearing Muddy rolled up at the Sea Life Park's rear entrance. Muddy was lowered gently into the water and James and other rescue team members joined him to literally walk him around, each of them willing the weak dolphin to take the initiative and begin swimming under his own steam.

He finally did so after two hours, but he was clearly still very weak and at first kept bumping into the sides of the big pool. Fortunately these had been padded with polystyrene and a toughened synthetic lining, which prevented Muddy from injuring himself further.

It was five days before he accepted solid food, however, and in the meantime he had to be tube-fed on fluids and force-fed the occasional fish. His breathing, monitored round-the-clock, was often laboured. Sometimes he literally threw back his head as if gasping. In fact James discovered on his second and more thorough medical examination of his new patient that Muddy had contracted a mild dose of pneumonia.

It was an anxious first week, during which Muddy appeared to throw in the towel on at least three occasions. He simply stopped swimming and sank slowly to the bottom. But, weary though they were from long hours spent watching Muddy's steady circuits, his

RIGHT Diver Alan Stuart lends James a hand in giving Muddy another check-up.
BELOW At long last … Muddy begins to swim on his own.

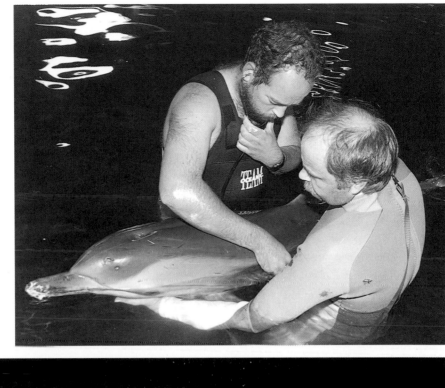

guardians were less ready to admit defeat, and within seconds he was hoisted back to the surface and set back on course. From the end of the first week onwards, however, Muddy's recovery gathered momentum. It was almost as if he'd told himself, 'Well all right, then, if you're not going to let me go quietly I'd better make an effort.'

His appetite improved and his weight increased steadily. Daily health checks confirmed that his lungs were clearing and his breathing pattern remained regular. James and others spent brief periods every day snorkelling alongside him, forcing him into short bursts of speed which gradually improved his strength. By the end of the second week he was well enough recovered to begin growing bored with his surroundings. A beach ball and other inflatable toys aroused his interest for a short while, but he was now clearly itching to get back in the sea. Indeed James was confident Muddy was now fit enough to be granted his freedom again, but his liberation was delayed another few days by bad weather.

The release operation had been carefully planned well in advance. A high-speed 'rigid hull inflatable' boat was to stand by about 100 metres distant, as close to Weymouth's pebble beach as it could get. Muddy would be transferred by van from the rear of the Sea Life Park to the coast road, then bodily lifted and carried across the beach in a canvas hammock to be placed in the boat atop an inflated mattress.

However, such was the level of media interest in Muddy's final farewell that arrangements had to be made for a second identical boat to carry journalists, cameramen, a few more divers, and last and quite probably least — me! I was certainly the least prepared for the trip, having assumed that both boats would actually be hauled just out of the water.

When all other preparations had been made and the boats were ready and waiting, a chain was winched down into Muddy's pool and a sling attached, into which Muddy was then carefully guided. The chain was cranked up, and a huge balance employed to weigh Muddy. His weight had increased substantially and steadily over the previous week, and when James then gave him a final medical check his physical health appeared excellent.

A team of eight carried Muddy to the back of the waiting van, where he was wrapped in damp towels and the skin around his blowhole smeared with KY jelly. Everyone on foot dashed across a grassy banking and across the coast road to wait for the unloading process. The van pulled up, people and dolphin piled out and within three minutes the first boat was fully occupied. It was at this point that yours truly realized with horror why almost everyone was wearing a diving suit. Neither boat was actually on the beach, but even so a strong leap at roughly that juncture would probably have seen me aboard safely.

Unfortunately one of the three TV crews chose that precise moment to insist on a few words 'to camera', with all the drama of boat-loading and shouted instructions happening in the background. Having obliged with the first words that came to mind, I turned around to find the second boat — the 'press boat' — a good 7 metres from shore, and the boat with Muddy aboard already powering out to sea. The helmsman on the second vessel was certainly not going to hang about much longer, so there was nothing else for it. I just walked into the sea, wondering as I did so where I might find a de-desalination recipe for a good pair of chord trousers and an equally decent pair of leather shoes.

It was a bumpy ride, too. If you've never surged through the waves aboard a throaty RHB before, take my advice … stick to pedalos. At least the buffeting served to take my mind to some extent off the clinging dampness and rapidly declining temperature from thighs downwards.

Five miles out to sea both boats cut their engines and two of the British Divers contingent slid over the side. Muddy was then tipped after them, and immediately began to swim. Unlike Spirit, however, Muddy took a long while to re-acclimatize. For half an hour he swam in slow circles, then began to gather momentum and to take occasional short dives. The ebb-tide drew him slowly but surely further out from land and finally, almost a full hour after entering the water, he started to swim strongly towards the distant horizon.

Away goes Muddy, much to the delight of onlookers.

The sun was low in the sky, and Muddy aimed straight at it. Only

by shielding eyes and squinting could any of the rescuers catch the occasional glimpse of his fast shrinking silhouette. It was the sort of moment which brings a lump to the throat. The kind of fairy-tale conclusion no-one ever really expects to experience in real life.

The fairy-tale was told that same evening to millions of engrossed children tuned into the BBC programme *Newsround*, accompanied by poignant footage of the entire release operation from convalescent pool to open sea. As the *Newsround* report closed with final shots of Muddy disappearing beyond the waves, the sun glinting on his smooth shiny back, happy smiles of warm approval must have beamed from young faces in living rooms the length and breadth of the British Isles. But was it really a case of 'happy ever after' for young Muddy? James Barnett was far from confident as he anxiously paced around Weymouth Sea Life Park in the hours following his return to shore.

James had been concerned by the marked difference between Spirit's sprint to freedom and Muddy's far more gradual departure, and no matter how often he turned over the facts of Muddy's recovered strength and health in his mind, there remained a niggling worry that perhaps he hadn't quite been back to his old self. That was why James was still in Weymouth instead of well on his way back to Cornwall. He had decided to stay the night just in case his discharged patient came back in with the next high tide.

Dawn found the local coastline liberally dotted with people checking for signs of Muddy's return, all fervently hoping to find nothing more than the usual collection of seaweed, timber and assorted human debris which tides wash up just about everywhere around our shores. No sign of any dolphins though; suitably encouraged, James finally set off towards the south-west. His doubts had not been ill-founded however, for it later became clear that Muddy had remained in the area after all. Most likely, he just needed a few more days of completely unrestricted exercise to build his stamina back to a peak.

Whatever the reason, there was certainly no doubting his fitness when he appeared suddenly close to shore at Portland Bill four days after his release. Swimmers in the area were both delighted and astonished to find a dolphin in their midst, but they later recounted that he was swimming powerfully and that he quickly vanished without trace.

I have a theory about this incident. It has no basis in science whatsoever and will be discarded by the majority, no doubt, as a wholly romantic notion unworthy of serious consideration. What I choose to believe, however, is that Muddy had spent the intervening period honing all systems and readying for what could only be a long journey and wide-ranging search to re-unite with other Striped Dolphins.

Once fully stoked up and raring to go, he was reluctant to do so without one final acknowledgement to the strange land animals that came to his aid in his hour of need. So he searched the coastline until he found a few familiar clumsy figures struggling through his own native environment with weird flailing limbs and sickly looking pale skin. The swimmers at Portland Bill would probably have been indistinguishable to Muddy from those other ill-adapted creatures that occasionally joined him for a swim in his pool at the Sea Life Park. Having located what he thought were his saviours, Muddy signalled a final 'thank you' with a triumphant sail-past, and then resumed his wild existence in earnest.

Just a theory of course, but it fits the circumstances rather neatly and keeps the fairy tale alive.

There was no further sighting of Muddy, and if he had perished — even if such a fate had occurred far out at sea — so numerous are the vessels patrolling the Channel beyond the coasts of Dorset, Hampshire and Devon that it seems unlikely we would not have heard about it.

No, he's out there somewhere. I wonder how long it would take a school of dolphins to swim from the Mediterranean to the southwest tip of Cornwall? Just over a week do you think? What if Muddy met up with those same dolphins I'd been watching …

The Oban Seals

When the surface of Loch Creran lies as still as glass, the sun picks out the purple heathers on the distant hills, and the surrounding woodland is alive with the chatter of birds, there are few more pleasant settings than the Oban Sea Life Centre, even in a region renowned for dramatic and idyllic landscapes.

The dark timber construction of the buildings helps them blend unobtrusively with the woodland background, and even the occasional shrieking laughter from children testing their agility in a small adventure playground seems not to detract from the general tranquillity.

The stunning view from Oban Sea Life Centre across Loch Creran.

ABOVE *Blondie glides gracefully past the underwater viewing window.*
BELOW *Behind this seal pup's doleful eyes are special reflective lenses which enable seals to detect even the faintest glimmers of light as they search for food in the murky depths.*

On days such as this, not even the hypnotic effect of a thousand silvery fish in shimmering circuit of the novel herring ring display can hold visitors indoors for very long, but when the public address system announces feeding time for the seals a crowd several people deep will gather instantly around the two outdoor seal pools, where resident Common Seals, Lorne, Blondie and Gigha will inevitably all be found vertical in the water, eyes facing the direction from which their guardian Terry Donovan will soon appear carrying a bucket of fish. At intervals the three resident seals share their quarters with younger animals in the final stages of recovery before returning to the wild, but even these short-term visitors quickly learn the routine, and they too know from which direction the 'waitress' makes her entrance.

Originally from London, Terry trained in marine biology and then qualified as a nurse, but she has never tended a human patient. She fell under the spell of one of the most graceful and endearing of marine mammals as soon as she first clapped eyes on the Oban seals, and has dedicated herself to their care and well-being ever since. Her southern accent sounds a shade incongruous as she begins her commentary, accompanied by the splash of greedy seals launching after fish, but her sincere affection for these animals shines through, and the audience is soon hanging on every word as Terry recounts the history of each individual seal, whether resident or rescued pup, describing moments of hilarity and some of sadness, revealing the individual personalities and nuances of each of her charges and throwing the odd question to spectators. The answers, right or wrong, enable her to paint a detailed picture of the Common Seal's lifestyle and biology, educational as well as entertaining — and with a serious underlying objective.

One or more of those in her audience may at some future date come across a seal pup somewhere along the coast or on the shore of a loch, and Terry hopes they will remember what they learned at Oban Sea Life Centre, and that their actions in the event of such discovery will consequently be in that young seal's best interests.

All too often in such circumstances people will assume the pup is lost or abandoned, while in the majority of cases the pup's mother will simply be away on a feeding sortie. But if she sees humans in attendance on her return she is unlikely to rejoin her offspring until they have gone. Terry advises to watch from a distance, and only after a long vigil has shown that the pup is indeed alone to then contact either the Scottish Society for the Prevention of Cruelty to Animals, or the Sea Life Centre.

Lorne, Blondie and Gigha are unquestionably the Centre's premier attractions, but ironically the rescue and care of seals had not even been considered when it was first built in 1979. The two events that changed matters occurred in quick succession in 1980, the first being the arrival of a tiny pup christened Patrick, thrust into the hands of bemused staff by an anxious holidaymaker who had found him on a beach somewhere and was convinced he was an orphan.

'We hadn't the first idea what to do with him,' recalls the manager of the time Mike Causer. 'He was clearly very young, possibly just a day old, and he still had traces of the umbilical chord attached to him.

'We certainly couldn't refuse to at least try and rear him, though. There was nowhere else he could go. So we settled him in the warmest spot we could find and began frantically telephoning round the country seeking advice on how to feed him and care for him. We even spoke to a couple of rescue centres overseas.'

Mike and his colleagues nursed the pup round the clock, and tried three or four different suggested food recipes, but, alas, to no avail. Patrick failed to respond to their best efforts, and slipped away within a few days.

'We were all extremely upset,' recalls Mike. 'The little chap had captured everyone's hearts and our inability to save him made us all feel so helpless.'

These days the Centre's care programme and facilities ensure a fighting chance for every pup that comes along, but even with all the knowledge and experience gained over fourteen years of rescue work, pups as young as Patrick was may still occasionally prove too frail to be saved. Fortunately, the next pup to arrive at the Centre — within a few weeks of Patrick's death — was a few days older. She was given the name Sally, and this time, with a lot of help and advice from a scientist at Dunstaffnage Marine Laboratories, who had succeeded in rearing a stray seal pup himself, Mike and his colleagues managed to rear Sally on a diet of glucose and sprats.

It was not long before Sally was happily splashing around one of the Centre's circular fish quarantine tanks, filled to a depth of about a metre, but as she continued to grow Mike quickly realized that new and better facilities would have to be provided for her if she was to remain at the Centre … and Sally was so dependent on her human keepers that a return to the wild was not considered a viable alternative.

'We were going through a learning process,' said Mike. 'In our enthusiasm and determination to keep Sally alive the last thing we worried about was the level of inter-action she was having with humans. Although work had been done with Common Seals elsewhere in the UK, the whole business was still very much in its infancy, and rescue, rather than rehabilitation, was very much the first priority.

'Seal pups are so cute it's easy to forget that they are wild animals and should not be treated too much like a pet. That was the trap we fell into, and there's no doubt in my mind that Sally just wouldn't have been able to cope in the wild.'

A fact that left the Sea Life Centre with little choice but to invest in providing Sally with suitable living quarters, and in the winter of 1980/81 work started on the first of the Centre's spacious outdoor seal pools so familiar to visitors today. By early spring of 1981 it was ready.

'I remember the day as if were yesterday, when Sally was first introduced to her new accommodation,' Mike recalls. 'She slid over the edge and launched straight into a complex underwater ballet. She packed just about every possible manoeuvre into a show which left those of us watching from the sidelines absolutely spellbound.'

As that work had progressed Mike and his recently arrived new colleague, Grant Stenhouse, had been scouring Britain in search of a possible companion for Sally, even though they guessed correctly that other young casualties would soon follow straight from the wild. They learned that another female pup, roughly the same age as Sally, had been successfully reared at the Suffolk Wildlife Park in Lowestoft after being found apparently abandoned on the coast of The Wash. The Wildlife Park had no suitable long-term facilities for their pup, and agreed to have her travel north to join Sally. That East Anglian pup was none other than Blondie, first of a trio of seals that were to grow from infancy to full maturity at Oban Sea Life Centre, and to make a lasting impression on visitors not only from all over

Scotland and the British Isles, but from as far afield as the USA.

Sally and Blondie greeted each other with some initial suspicion. Perhaps their memories of their own mothers and other seals they had been born among had by now faded to the extent that they believed themselves the same creatures which had fed and cared for them for so long. That confusion soon gave way to joyful exuberance, however, as Sally led a guided tour of her watery playground.

'All the sweat and toil that had gone into creating that pool was repaid a thousand times over in those first few minutes. It was a moving experience which none of us will ever forget.'

The arrival of the following summer brought a fresh batch of sickly, stray and abandoned wild pups. The SSPCA was usually the first port of call for holidaymakers who found such casualties, and officers now knew where to send them

The first two pups to arrive that year, however, also failed to survive, and Mike and Grant grew more and more convinced that diet was the problem. A breakthrough came when a lady veterinary surgeon from the Sea Mammal Research Unit responded to a plea for help and travelled to the wilds of the Scottish west coast to see how she could assist. Sadly one of the pups passed away before she arrived, but the subsequent 'post mortem' she carried out provided a wealth of new knowledge which was to help the Centre formulate a new and highly efficient treatment programme for all those pups that followed.

They learned that the glucose element they had been advised to incorporate into the infant feed had the unfortunate side-effect of causing dehydration, and the sprats, being whole fish, could potentially contain harmful bacteria within their stomach contents. Mike had also been concerned about the practice of feeding whole solid fish, irrespective of how small they might be, to animals which would still be exclusively on liquids were they still being fed by their mothers. A Common Seal's milk is very high in fat-content, and with that in mind a new 'baby food' was devised comprised of liquidized herring fillets — also very fatty — mixed with salt water and a substance called 'Ionaid', which provided both glucose and essential irons. This new formula, coupled with the introduction of antibiotic tablets, was an overnight success.

Whilst fortunes with the new pups took an immediate upturn, however, concern was growing about Sally. Behaviourally she seemed fine, but her coat — instead of being silky smooth — was covered in unsightly bald patches, as if she were permanently in moult. A procession of vets checked her over, but could find no obvious reason for her condition. Some suspected she was troubled with mites, and from time to time she was prescribed an assortment of different treatments, none of which seemed to make any difference.

Early in 1982 tragedy struck. Sally fell suddenly and mysteriously ill and none of the emergency ministrations of vets or staff managed to revive her. Within hours she had gone, and, needless to say, Mike, Grant and the rest of the Oban team were devastated. A post mortem failed to identify a specific cause of death, but the likelihood was that the deficiencies in her diet in the early days had left her with long-term internal problems, possibly aggravated by some of the medicines prescribed for her skin troubles. It was nobody's fault. Every course of action had been taken with the best of intentions … but that did nothing to lessen the grief of all who had known Sally, and had come to regard her as one of the family. It was she, more than any other seal, who had been responsible for the establishment of what grew to be one of the leading and most successful rescue and rehabilitation centres for Common Seals in Britain, a legacy which has to date saved the lives of well over thirty pups which found themselves in similar predicaments in their first tender days. A legacy that was also to result many years later in happy events which made all the heartache and frustration of the early days well worth the cost: events that involved the two seals that next found salvation in the practised hands of the staff at Oban Sea Life Centre.

It was June of 1983 when Grant Stenhouse received a call from the SSPCA which was to send him on a journey to the east coast, to meet a seal which had been adopted by children who came across her as they were playing on the beach at Broughty Ferry near Dundee. It had followed the children to a nearby paddling pool.

Blondie takes a nap. Note the pale complexion which gave her her name.

Grant christened the pup Gigha (pronounced 'gear') and even though she was very tiny, she responded well to Grant's intensive care, quickly progressing from the new formula baby food to whole fish. Vitamins were cunningly concealed inside the fish to replace those lost through freezing and subsequent thawing.

With Gigha, as with virtually all pups, the transfer from liquids to solid food involved a period of force-feeding, during which Grant had to straddle the young seal gripping her tightly with a knee either side of her body, and forcing a fish down her throat until Gigha had little choice but to swallow. After a few days of suffering this sort of indignity, however, she began to swallow her meals without need for such encouragement, and it was at that point that Grant realized the battle was all but won.

Of course there were fears that unforeseen problems might occur later. That was only natural after the experience with Sally, but happily they proved unfounded, and Gigha — like Blondie — was to go on to live a long and healthy life.

Male pup, Lorne, arrived only a few weeks behind Gigha. Again he had been found stranded on the Scottish east coast, and the family that adopted him had been feeding him on sardines and condensed milk.

'It was a potentially lethal cocktail,' says Grant. 'Even untreated cow's milk is far too rich for Common Seals although Grey Seals have done quite well on it. Luckily we got to Lorne in time and he soon began to thrive on the special feed devised at the Centre.'

Like Sally, Blondie, Gigha and Lorne each received perhaps too heavy a dose of human kindness, and to this day depend upon their human guardians for their survival. Even so they are not, strictly speaking, held captive, and could, if they so decided, simply slip down the banking alongside their pools and from there scuttle across the rocks just thirty or forty metres to the waters of Loch Creran.

This view of Gigha shows how streamlined seals are; perfectly designed for high-speed swimming.

Of the three of them, only Lorne has ever explored beyond the boundaries of the outdoor pools, however. Staff found him one morning sitting patiently in the staff car-park, and subsequently deduced that he had first been down to the Loch's edge then worked his way inland again, possibly having decided that Loch Creran was far too big a challenge for a chap so fond of his creature comforts! He certainly seemed mighty relieved to be helped back into more familiar surrounds, and although Blondie and Gigha's vocal reception gave all the impression of a severe scolding, the three of them soon settled back into a playful game of 'tag'.

By now Grant and his fellow seal attendants had realized a different strategy was called for if rescued seals were to be successfully returned to the wild, and with all subsequent arrivals they resisted the powerful urge to mollycoddle, curtailing human contact as far as possible once pups had been successfully weaned from liquids onto solids.

The policy reached fruition in the summer of 1984, and in the Sea Life Centre's new purose-built hospital a roll of honour records the first beneficiary as being a pup called Mac, who swam back to freedom on August 16th of that year, followed by Bertha on August 24th, and Puss on August 31st. The list is now a very long one, featuring no fewer than 36 names as this story went to press, and the new hospital erected in the winter of 1993-94 has further increased the Centre's rescue potential.

Even these triumphs, however, paled against other events of the summers of 1991 and 1992, when Lorne, Blondie and Gigha — still as much adored and admired by staff as they had been when newly arrived — finally demonstrated that they were pups no longer.

It was on the morning of Sunday, July 14th, 1991, that Terry Donovan came across a small bundle in the grass just alongside one of the outdoor pools, and within hours tiny Fingal, as she was later christened by a young Centre visitor, was greedily suckling from her mother Gigha, and had already mastered the art of swimming.

In the months that followed staff and visitors alike marvelled at the strength of the bond between mother and pup, and at the obvious affection each held for the other as they lay side by side or nuzzled up to each other at the water's surface. Equally touching was the way in which Blondie accepted the new arrival, and in which Fingal accepted and returned her gentle caresses with both nose and flippers.

The only one left cold by all this canoodling was Lorne, who was definitely jealous of his new rival for Blondie's and Gigha's attentions, and who was subsequently banished to the adjoining pool until Fingal gained both size and independence. A short ranch-style fence held the disgruntled Lorne at bay and he would often be found

Male seal Lorne.

peering through the upright struts with a look suggestive of utter disgust. It was just a phase, though, and as Fingal gradually grew more agile and less inclined to shadow either Gigha or Blondie, Lorne was allowed to re-join his family and actually paid Fingal little heed.

It would be remiss of me, at this stage, not to mention another seal who shared Fingal's company, and that of Blondie and Gigha, throughout this period, a pup named Houdini, who had arrived at the Centre a year earlier and had been diagnosed as having an incurable and sadly terminal liver disease. All Terry could do for Houdini, whose condition halted his growth at about a third of full size, was make him as comfortable as possible and administer the pain-relieving medicines prescribed by the veterinary experts.

Though the difference in their respective states of health grew more and more marked with each passing day, Houdini nevertheless provided Fingal with the company of another youngster, and was always willing to join in a playful romp, even if he could sustain the pace for only very short periods.

He was a real character, was Houdini, and had earned his name with a special talent for escaping the isolation cubicle in which he was first nursed. In that cubicle he slept in an old orange crate with warm soft bedding provided to add a touch of luxury, and when he was finally transferred outdoors Terry wisely had the orange crate transferred with him, sensing that this inanimate and fairly tatty piece of woodwork had been accepted by Houdini as a surrogate parent.

The shrewdness of Terry's judgement was confirmed almost every morning thereafter, when, on making her early hour inspections of the seal pools, she would find that Houdini had somehow tipped the crate onto one of its narrow sides, and lay blissfully asleep on top of it. How he achieved this remarkable feat neither Terry nor anyone else could ever discover. He wouldn't do it when anyone was watching! Terry tries desperately hard not to consider any of her patients

RIGHT Fingal suckles from mum Gigha.
BELOW Terry Donovan with pup Houdini. Few pups of this size can be safely handled in this way ... but Houdini was always a big softy!

as favourites … but would probably be first to confess that with Houdini she lost the battle. His frailty brought to the fore all of Terry's nursing instincts and when finally his illness overtook him, she comforted him to the last, shedding more than a few tears in the process.

That heartbreaking episode came long after the starkly contrasting event of Fingal's release into the wild in the middle of March 1992 at a secluded location on the banks of Loch Fyne, an hour's drive from the Centre. Terry was unsure how she would greet the prospect of freedom, even though she had demonstrated her ability to catch live fish and had now become totally independent from her mother and other seal companions. In spite of these facts Terry still wondered whether, however slender they might now be, the bonds between Fingal and her friends at the Oban Sea Life Centre would prove sufficiently strong to counter the call of the wild.

She need not have worried, for the still waters of Loch Fyne cast their spell within minutes, and, encouraged by another young seal, Boomerang, who was released at the same time, she was soon just a tiny speck in the distance, heading straight towards an island in the middle of the loch which is known to support a wild seal colony.

It was an especially poignant occasion for a six-year-old boy, Findlay Ross, who by virtue of being both a SeaWatch member and

Young Findlay Ross watches from the loch side as Fingal heads for freedom.

the youngest recruit to Terry's Saturday morning activity club for Oban children, was permitted to watch and to help with the release. Fingal took with her a special coded tag which will identify her should she ever come into contact with people in the future. In fact every seal pup freed from Oban is fitted with such a tag, and only one has ever been seen again, thankfully having simply broken free on rocks, its owner long gone.

The following summer it was Blondie's turn to give birth, the dramatic moment witnessed by a honeymoon couple from Edinburgh. Blondie's pup was a healthy male, and was chistened Warren after the surname of the privileged newly-weds who watched his entry into the world.

Warren proved every bit as lively as Fingal had been, his growth rate astonishing in relation to that of rescued pups, an indication of the relative potency of his mother's natural milk compared with any

Blondie and Warren.

artificial substitute. From the outset Warren's attitude to humans, both staff and visitors, was a wary one. Terry never put the matter to the test, but she gained the distinct impression that Warren would not have hesitated for a moment to bite the hand that fed him. Fingal, whilst far from tame, had been considerably more trusting. Terry realized, however, that Warren's behaviour was more akin to that of truly wild seal pups, a factor very much in his favour if he was join those wild pups at a later date.

The day came sooner than anyone expected. Anyone other than Warren, that is, for Terry was still busy making plans for his release when he decided to save her the trouble and saw himself off! Astonished staff caught only a final glimpse of his smooth profile angling purposefully across Loch Creran towards the coast and the islands beyond.

Sammy

Not all marine life resides in the sea itself, as any youngster who has ever explored a rock pool will happily confirm.

As a general rule, anyone intent on discovering sea creatures would find it a useful first step to head for the coast, though of course there are some sea fish that migrate up rivers to spawn and in Scotland, Common Seals often colonize lochs a long way from the sea proper.

Anyone bound for an exploration of the marine environment in Lancashire, however, would scarcely place at the top of their list a small expanse of water more than two miles inland known as Marton Mere, a reed-fringed fresh-water flash well known for its waterfowl and visiting migrant birds, but certainly not renowned for its sea creatures.

Imagine the surprise then, of a family enjoying a short weekend break at their caravan at the adjacent Marton Mere Caravan Park, when on emerging for an early morning stretch they were greeted by the doleful eyes of a very sorry looking Grey Seal pup. There must have been a great deal of rubbing of eyes and possibly a quick re-count of the previous night's empty wine bottles before the reality of the situation sank in. Then of course, there was the problem of what, if anything, to do about it.

Happily the family contacted the RSPCA, whose officers took some convincing that they were not dealing with a hoax call, but who nevertheless made for the scene as quickly as they could. And there, sure enough, lying quietly on the grass between the ranks of caravans, was a skinny Grey Seal pup. Neither of the two RSPCA officers at the scene would have claimed any great experience in dealing with seals, but a sick animal is a sick animal … and neither was in any doubt that here was indeed, a sick animal. The pup was too weak to raise any kind of protest at all as they carefully manoeuvred her into

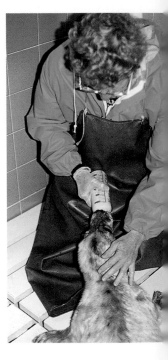

Rescued pups often have to be bottle-fed to provide the nourishment they need in the early days of their care.

Sammy now well on the way to a full recovery.

a large 'pet carrier', and then into the back of their van.

They then put a call into headquarters, who in turn alerted Rod Haynes, curator of the Blackpool Sea Life Centre, who despatched assistants to begin preparing one of the Centre's large circular quarantine tanks to accommodate the in-coming pup, before himself putting a call into the Centre's consultant vet.

Rod had spent a brief period years earlier helping with the seal pups at Oban, but they had been Common rather than Grey Seals, so he needed some advice. In the short term the seal was introduced to a tank with just a shallow measure of water in the bottom and a dry platform to lie on.

Of course all the Centre's staff popped in to see the new arrival within the first hour or two of her being settled in, but at this stage not even her gender had been determined and it was not altogether surprising therefore that she was given the name Sammy. There were some half-hearted attempts to introduce the alternative 'Samantha' once a more thorough examination had taken place, but these were politely ignored.

Sammy was in no condition to take exception in any case. The vet's check-up revealed a dose of pneumonia — which accounted for her laboured breathing, and a heavy infestation of parasitic lungworm. Of equal concern was the fact that Sammy weighed a meagre 18 kilos. At an estimated three months old, she should have been a hefty 35 to 40 kilos.

During her first 24 hours at the Centre Sammy was kept under close observation to ensure there were no adverse reactions to emergency medication administered to counter the pneumonia and lungworm. Thereafter it was simply a matter of fattening her up on a diet of herring.

There still remained the mystery of how Sammy arrived at Marton Mere; that was finally resolved by Paul Wiggins, of Skippool, on the River Wyre. An article about Sammy's rescue in the *West Lancashire Evening Gazette* was of particular interest to Paul, who quickly contacted the paper to help put an end to speculation. Paul believes he was the first to spot Sammy when he came across the seal struggling along the roadside outside a restaurant next to the river. He bundled her into a boat and took her out into midstream where he then fully expected her to head with the current back towards the open sea. Instead she turned around and swam upstream.

'Perhaps she assumed the current was just the tide,' he said. 'She had a lot of trouble swimming because there was a very fast flow and I thought she was going to exhaust herself.'

But Sammy finally began to make progress when she changed tactics and tackled the current underwater, rather than at the surface. Mr Wiggins eventually lost sight of her when she had reached a distant sewage pumping station. He assumed she would then have been forced to try the opposite direction, when she found her way barred, but after reading the *Gazette* story the next day, he realized that she must have slipped under the sluice gates and turned from the river into a narrow dike which runs two miles almost due south, ending at Marton Mere. Until Mr Wiggins had told his story, the only plausible theory anyone had come up with was that Sammy had simply been picked up by someone on the shore, driven to Marton and then dumped. It was plausible because, however senseless it might seem, similar things have happened in the past.

Even had Sammy been found on the Blackpool shoreline, however, it would still have been a notable event, since seals of any kind are an uncommon sight off that particular stretch of coastline. The nearest Grey Seal colony is at Walney Island, near Merseyside, and it is here where Sammy is assumed to have been born three months prior to her misadventure in the River Wyre. It was probably the combined effects of her twin ailments that drove Sammy towards the shoreline and unwittingly into the estuary of the River Wyre, where some blind instinct kept her moving steadily further and further from the sea, a course which, quite by chance, proved to be her salvation.

Whatever else she got wrong, Sammy's timing could scarcely have been better, for within a couple of weeks of her arrival at Blackpool Sea Life Centre the news was announced that the Cornish Seal Sanctuary had been welcomed under the same company umbrella, and arrangements were swiftly made to have Sammy transferred to the ideal facilities at the Sanctuary just as soon as she was fit enough to travel.

Sammy spent many hours lazing on the ramp down into her isolation pool in the Seal Hospital.

The transfer took place early in March, a much more boisterous Sammy now needing to be handled with far greater caution as she was bundled into a large 'pet carrier' and carried to the Seal Sanctuary van, parked on the famous Golden Mile.

James Barnett took charge of her recovery from then on, and Sammy made dramatic progress. She spent only a few days in the indoor hospital before moving out to join other recuperating pups in the isolation pools. A few weeks later she moved into the larger convalescence pool, where she quickly established herself as a firm favourite with both staff and visitors. Like all seals, she had her own personality, and the unique thing about Sammy was her tireless curiosity with regard to humans. Whereas most other pups tend to be most intently interested in either each other, or food, Sammy had an apparently endless fascination for folk. While her pool pals chased each other, spat, snarled, growled or barked at each other, Sammy would perform the seal version of 'doggy paddle' standing upright in the water watching visitors watching her.

She was eventually judged well enough to return to the sea in mid-November of 1993, and was released at Poldhu Cove on the Lizard peninsula together with pups Jon and Mandy. Jon had been the last arrival at the Sanctuary from the previous winter's breeding season, having turned up on March 8th, suffering from malnutrition. Mandy had been discovered a while earlier hiding under a rhododendron bush at Sidmouth in Devon, which must have puzzled no end the local blackbirds and robins.

All three took to the surf enthusiastically, Sammy looking for all the world as if it had only been the previous day rather than almost a year since her escapade in Lancashire.

Photographs of the release were sent to the *West Lancashire Evening Gazette* in Blackpool so that all those who had read avidly of her exploits could learn of the happy outcome.

Needless to say, that was the last anyone saw of her. Whatever it was that so intrigued her about *homo sapiens*, she must have got it out of her system at Gweek, unlike another former resident of the Sanctuary named Gladys. Details of Gladys's stay at Gweek are now lost somewhere in the mists of time, but she herself has certainly never forgotten, for she re-appears frequently every summer to bark up at the Sanctuary's staff from the Helford river down below the seal pools, begging for a free and easy meal. She invariably gets her own way in the end. Lately Gladys has begun bringing company with her, in the shape of two or three other seals who are no doubt mighty impressed by Gladys's unorthodox but effective feeding technique. Staff are keeping a close check on members of her entourage, but thus far they are pretty certain Sammy has not been among them.

Freeloader Gladys arrives alongside the Sanctuary to cadge another meal.

Courtney and Duchess

Courtney feeding one of the Seal Sanctuary's residents.

There are many common threads woven through all the stories in this collection, but perhaps one shines more brightly than the rest: the kindness and devotion bestowed by a few individuals on animals they have cared for.

If one story were to epitomize the spirit and common passion of all such characters, however, it might well be the story of Courtney Eustace and a seal pup called Duchess.

Courtney spent the best part of half a century toiling on a forty-five-acre farm, tending a small dairy herd and sometimes a few pigs; early on in his career he developed a special flair with the farm's livestock, and became particularly adept at helping cows through difficult births. Word quickly spread about this special talent, and every calving season would see Courtney responding willingly to emergency calls from any or all of four neighbouring farms, as well as from his own.

A back injury finally forced Courtney into retirement, but one summer his son, Martin, was given a summer job helping to usher cars into parking spaces at the Cornish Seal Sanctuary, and, having nothing better to do at the time, Courtney went along to lend a hand. While he was there he met the then owner and founder of the Sanctuary, Ken Jones, who persuaded him to stay on over the winter. Courtney was assigned all manner of tasks during that first winter, but was able from time to time to help out with the feeding of the Sanctuary's resident seals.

He quickly grew very fond of these ungainly and often noisy sea critters, and found that he knew instinctively how to handle them. By the time summer arrived once more, Courtney had been placed in charge of their daily care, a job which also entailed giving talks to visitors at feeding times, introducing them to each seal in turn and describing a little of their backgrounds and individual personalities.

Over the course of the next seven years Courtney became almost as much of an attraction at the Sanctuary as the seals themselves. His affection for his strange adopted family shone through at each and every feeding session, and the seals seemed just as mesmerized by his colourful West Country accent as the visitors were.

His family grew steadily, so that prior to his retirement from the Sanctuary in 1993, he was looking after 14 resident seals, 3 Californian sea-lions and 3 Patagonian sea-lions.

Not even the most casual observer could fail to detect the affection behind each of Courtney's anecdotes: tales like the one about Spitfire, a huge bull seal who had a real nasty streak when Courtney first started work at the Sanctuary. To illustrate how much things had changed he would sidle up to Spitfire, stroke him and then shake his flipper. Scobie was another of his favourites, a real character who signalled requests for food by noisily beating one flipper against his bulky chest.

Courtney was only once seriously injured by a seal, as it tried to snatch a fish from his hand and inflicted a wound requiring seven stitches. He is convinced that the seal responsible realized its mistake in the nick of time, and that that is the only reason why he still has all his digits. There was actually one other biting incident, but this more an example of mischief rather than an accident or any act of aggression.

'I was bending over to throw a fish into a pool when one of the female sea-lions nipped me on the backside,' he recalls with a grimace. 'Then she looked all around as if to say, "who, me!"'

Courtney cites a firm hand, kindness and the ability to show no fear as the necessary qualifications to work with adult Grey Seals and massive sea-lions. The sight of two tons of ravenous male seal heaving straight towards him doesn't phase him in the slightest. Unless of course the seal in question happens to be the infamous 'Bobbing Harry', the only Sanctuary resident Courtney could never quite bring himself to trust completely. A resident of over twenty years, Harry seems still to bear a grudge against all humanity, which is scarcely surprising since his arrival at the Sanctuary resulted from somebody shooting him in the head.

Although Courtney's duties involved him primarily with the adult animals at the Sanctuary, he helped out with many releases of seal pups, and savoured such occasions as much as any of his colleagues. One release in particular provided him with his most treasured memory. That was the release in the spring of 1993 of a pup named Duchess, a pup whose life was very nearly snatched from her before it had ever truly begun.

On February 23rd, 1992, Courtney was busying himself among his strange adopted family when he noticed that a pregnant female seal, Jenny, appeared to have gone into labour. After watching her for some time he realized that something was wrong, and, after first ensuring that Jenny was segregated from the other seals to prevent interference, he called on his many years of experience as a farm hand to assist the birth. Sensitive to Jenny's every anguished moan, he gently explored to find the cause of her distress. As he suspected, the pup was in 'breach' position, but with consummate skill and patience Courtney gently manoeuvred the foetus until he was able to draw it slowly out into daylight.

The tiny fur-covered bundle which then lay at his feet was entirely lifeless, but, having got this far, Courtney was not about to let it pass into oblivion without a struggle, and he began briskly massaging the

BELOW Pregnant seal Jenny is clearly in some discomfort. BOTTOM Duchess stretched out and enjoying a bit of warmth in the Seal Hospital.

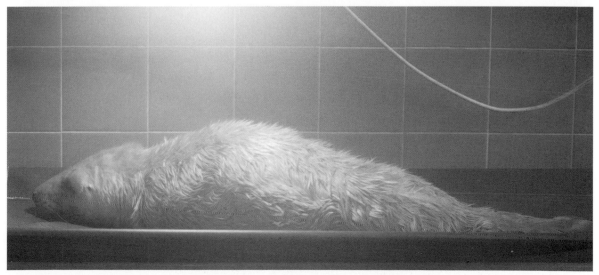

ABOVE *Duchess makes a swift recovery.*
LEFT *Loaded up and ready for release into the wild.*

pup in the manner he had sometimes used on stillborn calves. All this took place in full view of Sanctuary visitors, one of whom was recording the whole event on video. The small gathering grew still and silent as five, then six agonizing minutes passed without a flicker of a response from the bedraggled infant beneath Courtney's rhythmically stroking hands.

In fact it was ten minutes before the pup suddenly convulsed, took a huge gulp of air and raised its head to take a first look at the big wide world 'outdoors'. A spontaneous cheer went up from the onlookers, and Courtney leaned back against a convenient wall taking a relieved gulp of air of his own.

Ten minutes is an extraordinary length of time to elapse between

RIGHT The salt air and the sight of the open sea soon lure Duchess towards the tide edge. BELOW No turning back now.

birth and first breath, and doubtless many a midwife would have given up hope long before Courtney's determined efforts were successful. What convinced him that his ministrations were not futile after the first three or four minutes, only Courtney will ever know. Happily, the pup, subsequently christened Duchess, appeared unaffected by her troublesome introduction to life, and grew stronger and healthier day by day, under the proud and watchful gaze of her mother Jenny.

The video of Duchess's birth was presented to the Sanctuary, and is still relayed to this day to its thousands of visitors, Courtney's finest hour captured on celluloid and replayed over and over again to a steady succession of observers whose relief seems almost as palpable as it was first time around, when Duchess takes that vital first lungful of air.

On a pleasant spring day the following year, Courtney watched smiling as Duchess raised her snout to sniff the salt-laden breeze on a remote Cornish beach before ploughing into the surf and swimming strongly away to freedom. It was, without doubt, the most heart-warming moment of his long association with animals.

Myrtle the Turtle

Should you, in the near future, find yourself in the vicinity of Southsea, Portsmouth, you might care to call in to the Portsmouth Sea Life Centre and say hello to a lady called Myrtle.

If she is still there, Myrtle will most likely be found in the British sharks display, but Myrtle is the shy retiring type, so unless it happens to be feeding time you may have to look very closely into the darkest corner, where the Sea Life Centre's theming experts have cleverly fashioned an artificial cave from the realistic rockwork which gives this impressive tank an authentic 'under the sea' look.

She may have departed, of course, for Myrtle's residence at the Centre is strictly temporary. She has a rendezvous lined up with the Pacific Ocean off the West Coast of the USA just as soon as marine experts receive word that a nasty virus affecting many of her wild cousins has finally been eradicated. Myrtle's present guardians could not bear the thought of her returning to freedom after so many years of tender care, only to fall victim to some merciless micro-organism of the deep.

Were she human, instead of a turtle, Myrtle might well have been either locked up or expelled when her presence in the UK was first detected in 1986. All of the world's giant sea turtles are on the endangered list, with strict international regulations prohibiting their sale or capture, so Myrtle, who was then just a youngster measuring only seventeen or twenty centimetres long, was an illegal immigrant. A Pacific Green Turtle, she is thought to have first entered the country accidentally as a much tinier hatchling hidden in a consignment of tropical fish bound for an Essex garden centre.

Following a tip-off, a team of specialist customs officers, led by Southend man, Phil Birkett, descended on the garden centre in 1986 and took Myrtle into custody, only then to be faced with the

Myrtle pictured in 'quarantine' at Blackpool Sea Life Centre.

problem of finding her a more suitable home. They found one at Morecambe Marineland, in the popular aquarium alongside the out-door pools where Rocky the dolphin was at that time still a regular performer, but even the experienced Marineland keepers were astonished at Myrtle's alarming rate of growth over the next five years.

They had already begun investigating to find a more spacious home for Myrtle, when the sad decision was taken to place the ailing Morecambe attraction in the hands of receivers, and HM Customs and Excise were informed that their turtle would have to be re-housed as a matter of urgency.

Customs official, George Oxendale, contacted the newly opened Blackpool Sea Life Centre, and it was to here that Myrtle was first removed in 1991, but although Blackpool had an ideal display tank — a heated 100,000 gallon tropical display — the residents of that display already in situ might not have provided ideal company. They were a variety of tropical sharks ranging from Black Tipped Reef and Leopard Sharks just over a metre long, to a huge two-metre Sand Tiger Shark. Sharks are one of the few natural enemies of sea turtles, and although it is quite feasible that the well fed Blackpool sharks would have posed no threat to Myrtle, the risk was considered an unwise one; in any case it proved unnecessary.

The older Portsmouth Sea Life Centre had at least two displays suitable to accommodate Myrtle, and so she was soon removed from one of Blackpool's large quarantine tanks to begin the motorway journey south, throughout the trip constantly washed down with salt water to prevent harmful dehydration.

As it was late summer Myrtle was first installed in Portsmouth's stunning Deep Sea Discovery display, which at over four metres deep was the deepest aquarium tank in Europe on its construction in 1986 … round about the same time as Myrtle was first moving into Morecambe Marineland. The summer sun had raised the external sea temperature sufficiently to enable Myrtle to dive in comfort to depths she had never previously explored, since the water for the display was drawn directly from the nearby Solent, though it was held up en route to be subjected to a complex cleaning and filtration process. For the first time since her formative months in Essex she was not alone in her watery home, for she shared the Deep Sea Discovery with shoals of giant bass and bream, and a few sleek and menacing looking conger eels.

Myrtle seemed genuinely appreciative of the relatively wide open spaces offered by her new domain, and wasted little time exploring every inch, diving far deeper than she had ever before been able to dive, and examining her new room-mates with obvious curiosity.

Myrtle's arrival meant a change to the feeding routine for this particular Sea Life display, for the other creatures in Deep Sea

Myrtle explores the depths at Portsmouth Sea Life Centre.

Discovery were meat-eaters, their diet comprised chiefly of squid and mackerel, whereas sea turtles are mainly vegetarians.

After a few weeks, however, the Centre's displays staff noticed a surprising phenomenon, and one which appeared to be causing Myrtle a good deal of annoyance. The bass and bream had started tucking into Myrtle's lettuce leaves with relish, and, contrary to expectations, seemed to be thriving on this highly unorthodox fare.

Green turtle or not, Myrtle was thoroughly browned off by the whole business, and tried to chase off any fish that came in range of her meals, only to leave the way open, of course, for any other opportunist to then nip in and take a munch while she was suitably distracted. Fortunately dissent only set in at meal times, and for the most part Myrtle got on famously with her fishy co-habitants.

The arrival of winter necessitated another move for Myrtle to the slightly smaller British sharks display, where the water is kept warm and where none of the incumbent predators were of a size likely to pose any threat to her well-being. Indeed it might have been the other way around, for several of the sharks have felt the strength of

Myrtle's powerful jaws when they have attempted to come between her and her intended lunch. Luckily minor wounds heal even more quickly in sharks than they do in most other fish, and for most it was a case of 'once bitten, twice shy'. Myrtle adopted a novel solution to the problem of having to share her greens, and began happily consuming the fodder intended for the sharks. It has certainly not done her any harm, for in her time at Portsmouth she has grown from a hefty 18 kilos to approximately double that size in the space of two years.

An investigation was launched soon after her arrival there to determine the prospects for her return to the wild, spurred by news of the successful release of two other captive-reared Green Turtles off the coast of Florida that same summer. Both had been tagged for future recognition, and remarkably were spotted just four weeks after release, grazing on seaweed off the coast of Mexico some 1,000 miles further south.

Myrtle is still legally a guest of Her Majesty's Government; any future plans for her require the blessing of the Department of the Environment, but DOE officials were only too happy to endorse Myrtle's liberation plans once they had been informed of the Mexican sightings.

Sadly it was while Myrtle's emigration arrangements were still in the early planning stages that environmentalists first discovered the virus ravaging the wild population of Green Turtles. Her departure from Portsmouth was placed on hold, and at the time of writing was no nearer resurrection. The delay is causing more than a slight worry about the scale of the operation when finally Myrtle is cleared for take off. It may take a crane to hoist her from the water, and her accommodation in even the cargo hold of a Jumbo jet might not leave a great deal of room for ordinary luggage.

The delay did, however, enable customs man, Phil Birkett, to enjoy a touching reunion with Myrtle in March 1992, when he called in with colleague George Oxendale, who had arranged both Myrtle's first temporary home at Morecambe and subsequent move to Southsea. George had never actually seen her, despite devoting long hours to ensuring her suitable care; he was clearly as moved by the encounter as was Phil, who was quite literally staggered by Myrtle's increased stature. Both men helped displays manager, Lee Marshfield, to feed the hungry turtle from a perch above the shark display, and were soon left in little doubt as to why she had grown so substantially.

Myrtle was a celebrity long before anyone had heard of those fictional mutants with classical names and a diversity of martial arts skills. It seems certain she will continue to grab the limelight long after Leonardo and the rest have been very firmly consigned to the closet along with the hula-hoops. I suspect that when freedom does finally beckon for Myrtle, not even the infamous Shredder, arch enemy of the Ninja Turtles, would wish to get in her way.

*Customs officers George
Oxendale* (right) *and Phil
Birkett visit Myrtle at
Portsmouth.*

Goodbye Shirley and Valentine

There are surprises laid up by the score for anyone first embarking on an investigation into life beneath our seas.

Take the humble Cuckoo Wrasse, for example. You might reasonably conclude that a species that produces only female offspring would be destined to enjoy a very brief existence indeed. Not so. In fact the male-to-female ratio is consistently ideal, for whenever there are too few males about a female will simply undergo a sex change.

In its female form the salmon-pink Cuckoo Wrasse, with its few aesthetically positioned dark spots, is already considerably more colourful than most of our native sea fish, but when it switches to become a male, the necessary and complex biological changes are accompanied by an equally amazing transformation on the outside. Iridescent blue-and-orange waves appear along part or sometimes the whole length of the body, creating a pattern which is unique to every fish, and even the shape alters to become slightly bulkier, and more masculine.

It seems that many of the most astonishing phenomena in the oceans are associated with the business of procreation. Sex changes may not be too common, but there are countless examples of what would certainly be regarded as role reversal when viewed in traditional human terms. A classic is that involving Seahorses and their close relatives, the Pipefish, in which the females lay their eggs in a pouch on the male's abdomen, so that it is he — some weeks later — who effectively gives birth.

Even the lowly Fifteen-Spined-Stickleback performs minor miracles in the reproductive field. The male builds a nest platform between strands of weed, then, once the female has dutifully deposited her

ABOVE *A male Cuckoo Wrasse.*
RIGHT *The amazing 15-spined Stickleback.*

bundle, he first applies his unique brand of fertilizer, then neatly ties the whole thing up in a virtually impregnable package. More astonishing still, he accurately predicts the moment of hatching, and a short while beforehand cleverly unties his package again to enable his tiny sons and daughters to swim free.

Pretty fantastic stuff, you may think; but there is one reproductive phenomenon which is even more bizarre yet — namely the way the gender of newly born sea turtles is determined. Instead of genes being responsible, it is the temperature at which the eggs are incubated that governs whether the emerging offspring are little boys or little girls.

In view of the fact that male and female turtles are practically impossible to differentiate by visual inspection, it is a wonder that this incredible nugget was ever stumbled upon in the first place. However it came to light, it was certainly a subject that fascinated Southampton University researcher, James Sutherland, who determined to try and discover what those crucial temperatures are that produce either males or females.

Whether a gentle simmer produces girls and a good roast produces boys, or vice versa is probably still uncertain, and anyway that is really not important in the context of this story. The point is that in order to carry out his investigation James needed some turtle eggs, and these were unwittingly donated by an errant female Loggerhead Turtle who laid her eggs on a secluded beach on the Greek island of Cephalonia, and who did so far too late in the summer (in September in fact) for them to stand any chance at all of hatching naturally.

These eggs were carefully transported to Southampton, where James and his research team separated them into a number of roughly equal sized batches to be incubated artificially all at marginally different temperatures. The experiment had a secondary objective; to learn whether artificial incubation could provide a practical solution to alarmingly declining numbers in the wild turtle population. It is probable that neither objective was achieved conclusively, since apparently only four turtles actually hatched out.

These were then adopted by University technician, Jenny Mallinson, who nurtured them lovingly for approximately two years, until they simply outgrew the biggest available aquarium tanks in the University's Oceanography department. Two were then re-housed by Plymouth Marine Laboratories and the other two by Weymouth Sea Life Park.

Jenny Mallinson was determined that they should all eventually return to the wild, however, and before long she had recruited the assistance of wildlife charity Care For The Wild, who agreed to try and raise the required cash. Since then, Care for the Wild has estab-

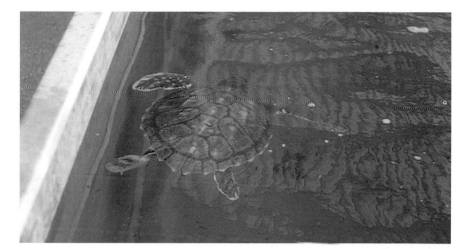

One of the turtles in an 'acclimatization tank'.

lished the Turtle Conservation Project in Sri Lanka, one of the few places in the world where five different species of highly endangered marine turtles come ashore to nest. The two turtles at Plymouth were christened Solo and Penta, the former reflecting its owner's independent nature and the latter a reference to the five-sided or pentagonal plates of a Loggerhead's shell, but as soon as plans for their to return to freedom in Greece were announced the Weymouth pair were promptly christened Shirley and Valentine … and the names stuck, for a while at least.

Jenny concluded that they would be mature enough to begin their return trip when four years old.

There was no way, however, that Shirley and Valentine could spend the intervening two years in the quarantine tank in which they were initially installed at Weymouth, for within a matter of weeks it became clear that both were taking full advantage of the extra space to do some very serious growing.

This may not entirely have been a result of space alone. Their new temporary keeper was Robin James, and he does seem to have an uncanny knack of prescribing diets for all his marine creatures that produce optimum expansion! When Solo and Penta were reunited with Shirley and Valentine at the end of two years, although also much larger than they had been on leaving the University, they weighed in several kilos lighter than the pair fed on the 'James plan'.

The happy reunion took place not at Weymouth, however, but at Brighton Sea Life Centre, where Shirley and Valentine had enjoyed the luxury of several of the biggest display tanks on the premises and attempted more than once — just like Myrtle at Portsmouth — to supplement their already ample diet with a slice of shark fin. They seemed to both revel in the company of other sea creatures and at the same time to resent it. On the one hand there was always a lot of activity to take an interest in, but on the other it was taking place in an area they appeared to consider ought to be for their leisure use exclusively.

Consequently they adopted a policy along the lines of 'if it shimmers and it moves faster than me, bite it.' Fortunately for those other creatures, just about every one of them moved a good deal faster than either Shirley or Valentine, and knew exactly when to use the accelerator to leave their frustrated adversaries snapping up beaks full of empty sea water.

What they did manage to eat fairly large quantities of was squid, and a variety of fish and shellfish, but evidently this fare did not include quite enough roughage, because in between meals they would feast on the filter bed, a deep layer of crushed cockleshell.

Care For The Wild, meanwhile, one of those charities that seems to get on with the job rather than promoting its image, had secured the backing of holiday company Thomsons and Britannia Airways to guarantee the four turtles passage to Greece. Jenny Mallinson designed special packing cases, custom-built to take into account the different sizes of the turtles, and a week before the scheduled departure Solo and Penta arrived to greet their long-lost kin.

The day came, and the four turtles were each weighed and measured before being transferred to their foam- and plastic-lined crates. Local TV cameras and a crew from the children's wildlife programme *Owl TV* recorded the event, with presenter Michaela Strachan among a number of enthralled spectators. More TV crews greeted them at Gatwick Airport, where the four curious packages were transferred out to the aircraft with minimum fuss. Several rows of seats had been taken out to enable the turtles to travel in the pressurized passenger compartment rather than in the cargo hold. It was felt the relative quiet and comfort of these surrounds would alleviate stress, as well as provide ready access for the two-legged travellers to tend to their strange luggage with a regular appliance of cool spray and damp cloths to prevent skin and eye damage.

One of those human attendants was Paul Hale, who had spent that summer working at Brighton Sea Life Centre and timed the term of his contract precisely to enable him to join this historic expedition.

'On arrival in Cephalonia the turtles were taken swiftly to a fish farm just south of the main town of Argostoli,' says Paul, 'where they were settled into a raceway used for rearing fish fry.

'Over the next week they were introduced to the local cuisine of fish, mussels and crabs and they were also taken for swims in the bay attached to specially made harnesses which allowed us to observe their behaviour without letting them wander too far.'

The larger pair, Shirley and Valentine, were chosen for release first, and a day beforehand were fitted with special radio transmitters,

Leo Durbin, Care for the Wild's radio tracker, attaches a radio transmitter to one of the turtles.

measuring 10 centimetres by 4 centimetres with an aerial about 15 centimetres long. These were actually glued to their shells and had a range of about nine miles. Reception was only possible when they were at the surface, however. Radio waves travel poorly through water!

On the morning of their release they arrived at the beach at Skala to be greeted by a huge reception committee of islanders, tourists, civic officials and local and international press. The turtles were unloaded while cameras rolled and clicked and were displayed briefly before the fascinated onlookers prior to being loaded onto a traditional Greek fishing boat. Local mayors, port policemen, turtle handlers, sponsors and journalists also clambered aboard. Then the heavily laden vessel trundled around the coast to the bay of

Potomakia, next to the very same beach from which those eggs had been unearthed four years earlier.

Photographers jostled for position as finally Shirley and Valentine were gently lowered into the sea, raising a loud and emotional cheer. I can't help wondering if either turtle experienced any feelings of an event long overdue as Jenny Mallinson and her university colleague, Ken Collins, captured some spectacular underwater video footage before the two turtles swam powerfully beyond camera range.

Two weeks went by with neither sight nor sound of either turtle, and then a call came through from a bemused windsurfer who had witnessed the uncanny sight of an aerial suddenly rising from the sea ahead of his board … like the periscope of a mini-submarine. He neglected to mention whether he had retained enough composure to avoid an unceremonious dunking, but project workers thanked him profusely and headed for the spot he described to them. Sure enough, after a bit of knob twiddling and delicate tuning, a steady blip was heard, indicating the presence of either Shirley or Valentine. The area was an extensive seaweed bed off the coast of a town called Spartia, and it was here that the team came across the larger of the two turtles alternately basking and grazing. Whether this was Shirley or Valentine is uncertain, because both had by this time been given different names, and the reports of this sighting refer to the re-located subject as 'Snappy'. They were probably both called by dozens of different names during their eventful first four years, and, as this latest pseudonym indicates, their temperaments were such that not all of those names may have been entirely complimentary. This contact, however, provided sufficient encouragement to initiate the release of the second two turtles, this time without accompanying radio gadgets.

These two were freed from Skala beach with a local schoolteacher and some of his children assisting, while hundreds of other schoolchildren from all over the island watched excitedly along with crowds of tourists.

'This release went without a hitch too,' says Paul Hale, 'and Solo and Penta quickly swam out to sea.'

The turtle now known as Snappy was tracked for another two weeks before contact was lost as he headed north, resulting in a sighting a little while later by another windsurfer at Vassiliki, on the south coast of the island of Lefkas. Two months after the releases a sighting of an aerial-toting turtle was received from a sailing club in the north of Cephalonia, and if one of them had survived this length of time it seems reasonable to assume that all four were probably coping well. Whether or not the project had been a total success remains to be seen, and there could be a long wait before the releases can be declared a complete triumph.

Final proof would be the return of one or more of the four to a beach on Cephalonia to lay their own eggs; but Loggerhead Turtles do not breed until eighteen years old at least, and often not until they reach thirty years. Solo, Penta, Shirley and Valentine each have a small durable identification tag attached to a hind flipper to reveal their identities should they indeed return. The latter pair's radio antennae should have fallen off after a few months at most. If they didn't, perhaps both are still grazing lazily on seaweed somewhere in the Mediterranean, listening happily to a Latin music station!

There is no reason to believe that these four hard-cased characters were any less well equipped for survival in the wild than their numerous cousins who did not enjoy a head-start in the safety of a captive environment; even if they had been, their release still would have served a vital purpose.

It focused the attention of Greek islanders on the biggest threat to the continued survival of an already precariously balanced species, namely the loss of so many of their traditional nesting beaches to tourism and other associated development.

That is why all those cheering crowds and hordes of schoolchildren were not only tolerated at the two releases, but actively encouraged, guaranteeing that Solo, Penta, Shirley and Valentine would win enough admirers to create a powerful incentive to ensure that undisturbed beaches are preserved for the day of their eventual return.

And that will enable hundreds of other mature turtles in the interim to struggle up from the water's edge, dig their nest holes and lay their eggs, to ensure the continuance of this creature whose loss to our oceans would be tragic.

Picasso

Though each has its own well defined range, the big sea turtles are all seemingly capable of travelling vast distances. The wanderings of Loggerheads, for example, are thought to take them from the Mediterranean to the Caribbean and back again, with these journeys usually taking place within a fairly narrow range band either side of the equator, determined of course by the sea temperatures that suit the turtles best.

Loggerheads are the most prolific species visiting the Mediterranean, and are thus, more frequently than other species, unwittingly sidetracked by the Gulf Stream, and both sightings and strandings in more northerly latitudes are virtually an annual event. These usually coincide with the migration of Loggerheads from west to east when some turtles fall foul of the clockwise rotation of the Gulf Stream around the Atlantic on their departure from the Caribbean. Most diverted turtles do manage to make some progress at angles to the current, with the result that strandings along the Irish coastline are far more frequent than those along the western shores of England, Wales or Scotland.

It must be a tiring business for even the strongest and healthiest of turtles. There was one, however, for whom the need to avoid the more irresistible currents of the Gulf Stream was far more critical than it was for the rest. That turtle, later to be named Picasso, had at some time fallen foul of either a boat propeller or more likely a hungry shark, and from the circular gap in his shell which should have accommodated a powerful right front flipper, there hung instead just a short and ugly stump.

His painful injury long since healed over, Picasso had gradually learned to compensate for the sudden loss of balance and symmetry, but his missing limb was to prove an almost fatal handicap when at

Picasso is finally freed, to resume his interrupted migration.

the end of the summer of 1991 he set out to make that epic annual Atlantic crossing.

He may not even have been aware at first that the Gulf Stream had him in its insistent clutches. For a week, perhaps two, he may have ploughed stubbornly on through the waves or beneath the surface certain of his bearings until gradually the warm current began to cool alarmingly as it converged with the shockingly cold waters of seas far to the north of his intended route. We can only guess that this is what happened, but subsequent events point to just such a scenario, or at least to circumstances very similar, and we can also only surmise that Picasso, on feeling those first icy tentacles, at last realized that he was far off course, and began vainly to fight for his life against that steady and unyielding watery battering ram pushing him ever further and further to the north. Many other Loggerhead turtles had tried and failed before him, and they had at least been in possession of all their limbs. For Picasso, the struggle was always destined to prove futile, but struggle he continued to do, weakening by the day, growing slowly colder and colder but always labouring eastward degree by agonizing degree, until at length with his strength finally failing and his lungs racked with pneumonia, he had nothing left to give. Close to death and utterly exhausted, Picasso drifted on the surface until his three surviving flippers suddenly caught and dragged at the sandy seabed.

Somehow Picasso summoned reserves for one final desperate bid to cheat fate, and dragged himself an inch at a time along the sand and out of the sea to lie exposed on an unfamiliar and rugged beach, a beach completely unlike that one across which he had scuttled at birth to seek the relative safety of the sea. How ironic that in his hour of direst need, it should be a beach, as opposed to the sea, that offered one last remote hope of salvation.

Picasso had come to rest in a tiny bay at the northern tip of the island of Coll in the Inner Hebrides. How long he lay there we will never know. What we do know, though, is that that tiny bay lies adjacent to the coastal route walked every Sunday afternoon by crofter Donald MacFarlane as he checks on the welfare of his sheep. Donald had trekked that windblown path more times than he cared to remember before one particular Sunday afternoon in October 1991, when a mysterious shape alongside the seaweed in the bay attracted his attention.

Making his way across the sand he realized while still many yards distant that the object was a large turtle, but there was no movement to indicate the animal was alive. Then when he was literally bent over Picasso, he could detect the faintest signs of breathing, and Donald quickly hurried back to his house to fetch something to carry him in. The only thing suitable was an old potato sack, with which he returned to the bay to retrieve his strange find. Picasso was too weak to raise even the slightest protest at such an undignified mode of transport.

Back at his house Donald consulted his father over what they should do next, and, sensing that Picasso's skin was drier and more brittle than it ought to be, they decided to first of all place him somewhere cool and damp. The shower basin seemed ideal, so that's where he went together with just enough water to cover his lower body and chin. As it happened, Picasso was dangerously dehydrated, and Donald's action was probably the most appropriate anyone could have taken in the circumstances. Making Picasso as comfortable as he could, Donald then retreated to the telephone to call the vet, Patrick Boyd, on the Isle of Tiree.

It was scarcely typical of the kind of emergency Mr Boyd might have expected on a quiet Sunday evening, and turtles were not exactly his speciality, but he needed only a moment's thought before recommending an appropriate course of action. And so Donald found himself making another call, this time to Terry Donovan at the Oban Sea Life Centre, who listened attentively to his account of the day's happenings while at the same time pondering the best way to get the turtle from Coll to the mainland.

'From Donald's description of Picasso's state of health it seemed certain he was in need of urgent help,' said Terry. 'I needed to get him to the Sea Life Centre as quickly as possible, but that was not going to be until the next day at the earliest, so I asked Donald to keep him damp, by covering him in seaweed, and to persuade the island ferry operators to ship him to Oban on the Monday.'

That is exactly what Donald did, and the following day Terry was waiting anxiously at the quayside to collect a fish box, in which Picasso lay, still tightly packed in damp seaweed. She opened up the box right there on the harbour to check her new patient's condition, and what she found offered her very little cause for optimism.

'He was very nearly comatose,' she recalls. 'There was no movement at all, and at first I wasn't even sure he was still alive. He had been out of the water for so long that his skin was turning black and one of his eyes was badly ulcerated and cloudy. His shell was also a bit damaged. Even when it became clear he was still breathing I must admit I didn't hold out much hope for him.'

Where there is life there is always some hope, however, and, as many creatures have learned to their benefit, Terry is not one to throw in the towel until every last effort has been exhausted.

She rushed Picasso back to the Sea Life Centre where a display tank had been cleared and equipped with a heater. She decided the fish box would make an ideal artificial island for the still unmoving turtle while allowing the water in the display to wash him gently as it seeped through the open sides, so she lowered both box and turtle into the display together. Gradually the water temperature was raised as Terry and colleagues watched patiently for any signs of recovery. For what seemed an age he lay frozen and seemingly oblivious to anything or anyone around him, but after two hours, with the water temperature now climbing over 20°, he at last raised one of his three surviving flippers and slowly turned his head as if to better take in his surrounds with his one good eye. Terry was elated, and by the time the vet arrived a short while later was actually daring to believe Picasso might be saved. It was Terry who christened him Picasso, the name inspired of course by the Ninja gang Leonardo and friends. It was an appropriate choice, for by the time she finally parted company with him Picasso had certainly become her own personal 'hero turtle'.

A vet was drafted in at short notice from nearby fish farming operation Golden Sea Produce, and, as luck would have it, earlier in his career he had been something of a specialist in the treatment of reptiles. He prescribed a special cream for Picasso's poorly eye, a spray to apply daily to his skin and to his damaged shell to prevent infection setting in there, and injections of antibiotics to be administered for the first few days just to bolster his own natural defences and help him recover from hypothermia.

Soon Picasso became so animated that Terry judged it safe to remove the fish box and grant him the freedom of the large hexagonal fish tank which was to remain his home for the next two weeks. She fully expected him to dive straight to the bottom, as turtles normally spend far more time submerged than at the surface. He did seem to try and dive a few times, but on each occasion quickly popped back up to the top again.

Leaving him to his own devices for a while, Terry began telephoning other Sea Life colleagues and animal specialists around the country in search of helpful hints, and was eventually put in contact with the Northern Ireland Aquarium at Portaferry, which, as a result of caring for no fewer than six turtles in the space of just three years, had become a kind of unofficial turtle rescue mission for the whole of the British Isles. A friendly and very helpful contact at Portaferry, by the name of Tania Johnston, offered Terry a wealth of useful advice, and was also able to solve the mystery of Picasso's seeming reluctance to stay underwater. This proved to be a phenomenon quite common among stranded turtles, and is a result of excess air creeping in beneath their shells.

It was not that Picasso did not want to go under, he simply would not be able to stay down until his body gained sufficient bulk to squeeze the trapped air out from beneath a more snug-fitting shell, a process which was to take the best part of a fortnight.

One week after his arrival at the Oban centre, Picasso accepted his first food, and, though picky to start with, he was soon consuming large quantities of herring, mackerel and — his favourite by far — squid. Terry also noticed to her delight that as his appetite was returning, the ugly blackened skin around Picasso's face, neck and flippers had begun to peel away revealing a fresh and pristine layer beneath. His eye was also responding well to treatment. Eventually — though of course he could never grow back a replacement front offside flipper — he looked almost as good as new.

Terry had grown convinced that the aquarium at Portaferry was the ideal place for Picasso to complete his recovery, especially as that aquarium, which has since been more than quadrupled in size and given the new name Exploris (short for exploration of the Irish Sea) had already successfully returned other rescued turtles to freedom off the coasts of Madeira and the Azores.

Next problem, how to get him from Oban to Northern Ireland?

This turned out not to be much of a problem at all. British Airways proved more than sympathetic to Picasso's plight, and agreed to provide him with a free flight. Terry was invited to go too, of course, which she duly did on November 6th, 1991, Picasso sufficiently improved by this time to put on a bit of a show for assembled journalists and TV crews at Glasgow Airport. Bearing in mind Picasso's sorry condition on arrival at Oban, it was amazing how fit and strong he now seemed. Indeed Terry was struggling to keep his powerful flippers from dealing her a nasty bruise or two as she raised him aloft on the aircraft steps while he flapped his port-side limb and waved a final salute at the cameramen.

BA had even allocated Picasso his own seat. A good thing too, because the size of his travelling case was such that had it needed to be perched between the aisles no-one would have been able to pass in either direction. During the short flight, Terry was able to moisten him regularly with sea water, which she had brought along in suitable spray bottles.

Terry accompanied him from the airport to Portaferry where she met Tania and the aquarium's assistant manager, Alistair Davison, the two people who were to share the job of looking after Picasso for what turned out to be another six months. Again he was assigned his own exclusive tank, and he continued to regain strength, weight and stamina day by day. Tania phoned Terry on a regular basis with progress reports, and Terry in turn would telephone Donald MacFarlane on Coll, who was following Picasso's fortunes with avid interest.

During the early days of his stay in Portaferry Picasso came under more veterinary scrutiny, and it quickly became apparent that the damage to his shell was even more serious than had first been diagnosed. It was discovered that rot had set in around the damaged areas and beneath the scar plaque which had formed on top of the worst affected part of his shell. Urgent treatment was needed to stem the decay.

After the soft and rotting material had been gently scraped away, a fairly deep hole was left measuring about 8 centimetres by 5 centimetres, and this needed to be packed and covered. Dental packing had been used for this purpose with earlier casualties, but for a wound of this size was considered too soft, too soluble and possibly too ineffective a barrier to further infection.

Epoxy resin had also been used previously with some success, but again Picasso's wound was too large to contemplate using a material which contains potentially toxic solvents.

Instead the Portaferry team used orthopaedic sterile bone wax which was donated by a local hospital, a white substance made up of 75 per cent bee's wax, 15 per cent paraffin wax and 10 per cent isopropyl palatate. Picasso had to be removed from his tank and dried thoroughly before this could be applied, but the whole procedure took only 15 minutes. The wax seemed to cement itself well to the dry shell and showed no signs of leakage. After 5 days it was removed to reveal that new tissue growth had appeared. On veterinary advice the area was re-treated with neobiotic ointment and re-covered with bone wax for a further 14 days.

When the wax was removed for the second time, Picasso's wound appeared to be almost completely healed, and continued to improve over the following three weeks until almost indistinguishable from the surrounding undamaged shell.

By the spring of 1992 Alistair and Tania concluded Picasso was fit enough to go home just a soon as suitable travel arrangements could be made. Having weighed only 10 kilos when first delivered to Oban Sea Life Centre, he now weighed just over 17 kilos.

British Airways again came to the rescue, flying not only Picasso, but two other turtles from an aquarium just outside Dublin to London, where the three of them spent a night at London Zoo. The following day they were flown out to the Azores by TAP Air Portugal, and then taken three miles off shore and released in the clear deep water of the Canaries Current, to continue their interrupted migration around the mid-Atlantic.

Picasso evidently took to the water with powerful strokes of his three flippers, and was soon lost to sight.

It took some while for the happy news to filter back to Northern Ireland, and from there to Terry Donovan at Oban, where it was greeted with beaming joy. When Donald MacFarlane was informed he was both amazed and delighted. He had never imagined that his anxious phone calls that Sunday afternoon nearly seven months earlier would trigger a rescue operation on an international scale, and each time he passes that pebble-strewn beach at the northern tip of Coll he must wonder to himself where Picasso might be now.

Personally, I would love to know whether he has bumped into Shirley and Valentine yet. If Loggerhead Turtles could talk to each other I bet all three would be holding court somewhere in mid-ocean recounting their bizarre experiences to a rapt audience. The question is, would any of those other less distinguished turtles believe a word of it?

A Splint for a Sunfish!

A frequent summer visitor to the seas around our south-west coast, though usually in numbers that can be counted on one hand, is the Sunfish: without doubt one of the most bizarre creatures in all the wide oceans.

A Sunfish looks like nothing else in the sea, or on land. Its body is shaped like a short chunky missile which has been compressed on both sides. The blunt rear end is fringed with a very short tail fin running from top to bottom, and just forward of this, both above and below, protrude two enormous fins which can be as long as the body, and shaped something like conventional aircraft wings. At the Sunfish's sharp end is an almost perfectly circular mouth ringed by very human-like lips, and just behind and slightly above the mouth, and on either side, are two huge eyes sometimes with a dull orange surround to their dark iris. The body colour is generally a blue-grey, and tends to be darker above than below. This may be a protective device and is common in a large number of fish. Pale underparts are thought to be less easily distinguished from light at the sea's surface by any hungry predator passing beneath.

Sunfish are grazing creatures, feeding on drifting plant and animal life a bit like the grazing whales, but it is not merely their appearance that makes them so extraordinary, as the crew of a large steamer, the *SS Fiona,* discovered to their cost when passing close to Bird Island, off the east coast of Australia on September 18th, 1908.

All of a sudden the ship gave a shudder which reverberated through its entire structure, and sent many of its crew tumbling to their hands and knees. The *Fiona* lurched to a grinding halt. It was evident to the startled seamen that something had fouled one of the propellers, though they could not imagine what it might be. There was nothing else for it but to take a look, so a couple of the strongest swimmers

The Sunfish, pictured at Weymouth Sea Life Park.

were duly lowered overboard, where they each filled their lungs with air and dived towards the stern. What they discovered, firmly wedged between one of the propellers and its housing, was one of the biggest creatures they had ever seen, excepting of course whales. Whether they knew it was a Sunfish or not is not detailed in the somewhat sketchy accounts of this episode which survive today. They certainly knew, however, that it could not be dislodged, and reported as much to their skipper.

The *Fiona* was then forced to limp some 40 miles to Port Jackson, Sydney, where the steamer entered dry dock at Mosman Bay. It took a whole day to remove the unfortunate fish from its fatal trap, after which it was heaved up on the dockyard scales and registered an incredible two and a quarter tons. It was 3 metres long and 4.2 metres high, from fin-tip to fin-tip. At the time it was the largest Sunfish ever recorded, but there have been subsequent sightings of individuals even larger than this, measuring 3.9 metres long and nearly 6.1 metres high.

In light of such proportions, it is perhaps not so surprising that an adult female Sunfish can lay literally millions of eggs, probably more than any other species. It is such a docile and slow moving creature that many of its offspring must fall victim to predators. Perhaps thousands actually survive to reach a respectable size of a foot or two in length, but it is doubtful that even at this size they can do much to determine where exactly they travel, being ill-equipped to put up much of a struggle against even the gentlest of currents.

Consequently many will be carried into inhospitable seas where they, too, will perish, until ultimately only a few will be left to reach maturity and begin the cycle all over again.

One of those unfortunate thousands which was clearly not intended to enjoy its full potential life span was a Sunfish of just less than a metre in length, which got caught up in tidal currents near the Weymouth coastline in late September 1992. It was found floundering in the shallows by a local fisherman, who delivered it a short while later to Robin James at Weymouth Sea Life Park.

Robin had dealt with Sunfish in the past, and had found them to be very receptive to a period of care and convalescence in captivity, but this one, he realized, was badly injured. The lower of its two fins was limp and twisted, and had clearly been damaged when it had come up against the unfamiliar and unyielding seabed during its struggles in the edge of the tide. Robin cleared a large quarantine tank for his new tenant, but saw immediately that its injury was hampering its movements, causing it to swim at an unnatural angle, and probably aggravating its wound with each attempt to right itself.

Thus it was that veterinary surgeon, Martin Fielding, was summoned to tend what was probably the most unusual patient he had ever encountered. Martin had faced some tricky assignments in his time, but this one was to tax his ingenuity as much as anything he had previously come across.

It was far less straightforward than a mere broken limb. The substance that gives a Sunfish's fin a degree of essential rigidity is not bone but a more supple material like cartilage. Rather than being broken, this was simply bent and misshapen. The fin could be straightened by hand quite easily, but would simply spring back into its distorted state once let go.

Martin was at first flummoxed. The obvious solution was a lightweight splint of some kind, but any conventional splint or cast would be too heavy and rigid, preventing the Sunfish from swimming adequately and probably causing it to sink to the bottom and inflict more damage to itself. Briefly, he considered an X-ray to find the full

Martin Fielding (right) *makes an inspection of the damaged fin with a bit of help from Robin James* (left) *and another Sea Life Park assistant.*

extent of the problem, and, though he dismissed the idea almost as quickly, it nevertheless prompted another thought which turned out to be the perfect answer. He left the Sea Life Park and returned a short while later with a sheet of X-ray film, which with Robin's assistance he cut to shape and bent around the leading edge of the damaged fin before stitching it in place on both sides.

Within hours the Sunfish was swimming almost normally again, still favouring its injured dorsal fin somewhat, but managing to maintain a vertical posture. Only time would tell whether the makeshift splint would do the trick or not, and in the meantime Robin still faced the always tricky task of nursing his subject through a period of inevitable stress and then persuading it to begin feeding and rebuilding strength and stamina for an eventual return to the sea.

Robin's skills in this department are, in the opinion of all those who have known or worked with him, quite simply unrivalled, and it came as no surprise to Martin when he returned to check on his patient a couple of weeks later, to find the Sunfish happily accepting food straight from Robin's fingertips. Robin often gives the impression that he could secure just the same trust and confidence from even a Great White Shark, were the need ever to arise.

Needless to say, Robin was overjoyed when Martin Fielding examined the splinted Sunfish and declared the afflicted fin as good as new. Off came the splint and off swam the Sunfish to demonstrate that total mobility control had indeed been restored. By this time an unprecedented event had taken place: a second Sunfish had arrived, again found caught in the shallows but this time suffering little more

The Sunfish's fin much improved.

than exhaustion and a mild parasitic infection. The two Sunfish were of course accommodated together, and before long were both fit and strong enough to move to one of the larger public displays at Weymouth, to join British sharks, stingrays, a shoal of mackerel, garfish and a few others.

As the weeks went by, their appetites grew until each was consuming an incredible 2 kilos of squid per day. Their physical growth was equally dramatic, lending gradually increased credibility to the text-book assertions of full grown Sunfish measuring 4 metres long.

Robin was keen that they should be allowed to reach the maximum proportions which any Sea Life display would facilitate before being returned to the sea, thus hopefully increasing their long-term survival prospects. Hence their transfer in June of 1993 to the Brighton Sea Life Centre to enter what was then the biggest marine life display in Britain, the gigantic 170,000 gallon display which had been converted from the old dolphin pool where Missie and Silver once lived. Within two months the pair had expanded to measure 1.2 metres tall from fin-tip to fin-tip, and this allowed them just enough room to pass comfortably above the underwater tunnel from which visitors watched their activities, sometimes wearing expressions of complete astonishment. That such creatures could actually occur in our own seas was clearly a matter of some surprise for many people.

Meal times presented new difficulties in this larger environment, however, with the resident sharks frequently poaching tit-bits intended for the two Sunfish, and eventually two of the centre's staff resorted to donning scuba gear and entering the display to feed the pair by hand again.

Ultimately even this tank was beginning to look a little cramped, and by September it was agreed the pair would have to go back to sea before they became too large to be moved.

The operation took place on September 28th and involved each Sunfish in turn being netted by divers, Justin Measures and Matthew Shepherd; loaded into a deep portable container filled with water; wheeled and hoisted into the back of a van; driven at two miles per hour to Brighton Marina and then winched into a second tank aboard an ex-naval tender ship now operating as a commercial divers' vessel. Twenty miles out to sea the fish were again winched out of their tank and gently lowered into the briny, where Justin and Matthew removed their harnesses and watched them slowly swim away.

By now, they may well be somewhere in the mid-Atlantic, perhaps lazing at the surface soaking up the sun's warmth in the manner that first earned them their name.

Given their phenomenal rate of expansion, I would guess that passengers spotting them from any nearby cruise ships would mistake them either for whales … or possibly even stray icebergs!

Barney the Barnacle

There can be few more unlikely celebrities than Barney the barnacle.

In his small display tank at Oban Sea Life Centre, Barney does ... well, nothing! He is about eight centimetres across and the same in height, but in all other respects he is no different from those much smaller acorn barnacles which everyone has seen encrusted on boulders or boat hulls, just about everywhere around the British coastline. It is not strictly true to suggest he does absolutely nothing. Occasionally some feathery tendrils will emerge from the small bill-like opening atop his shell, and waft gently around sifting particles of food from the surrounding sea water, and about once a year or so he will lose those feelers altogether, shedding them in favour of a brand new set which grow in their place; but that is all. He certainly does not actually move, and neither will he do so for the rest of his life unless assisted in the process.

Hard to imagine Barney becoming a major crowd puller, is it not? And yet for a few weeks in February 1993, after his arrival at the Centre, he was the most popular resident by far, more so than the seals even, and fully a year later he was still being regularly asked after, so effectively had word spread about this strangest of megastars.

It was not merely that he was the biggest barnacle to be seen in Britain, nor that he was the only one of his kind: no, it was the manner of his arrival that captured the public imagination, and encouraged folk from throughout Scotland and even beyond to pay him a visit and see for themselves the luckiest barnacle alive!

As already stated, most of us have seen plenty of barnacles, but I doubt many people — apart from those who have seen Barney — have ever found one bigger than a couple of centimetres across at most. Acorn Barnacles just do not get much bigger than that, and the real big guys like Barney prefer deep, deep water where they are so seldom seen by humans that they do not even have a common name.

When he arrived at Oban, Barney was already at least five years old, and could have spent those five years at a depth of anything up to 305 metres. Under normal circumstances, once having chosen a suitable rock to cement himself to, he would have stayed in the same spot on the seabed for good, with successive generations of barnacles growing around him and on top of him to form a large irregular cluster.

This practice tends to lead to the shells of these giant barnacles being anything but symmetrical, with growth stunted wherever a younger barnacle chooses to attach itself, but Barney had apparently not been as sociable as most of his brethren, and as a result was

Barney the Barnacle – firmly attached to his orange float.

commended by marine expert Dr Margaret Barnes, of the Scottish Marine Biological Association as a 'perfect specimen' of the species *Chirona Chirona Hameri.*

He was delivered to the Sea Life Centre by a family returning from a trip to the island of Mull, where they had found him on the seashore attached to an orange cork fisherman's float. They carried him with them back to the mainland out of simple curiosity, having never seen a crustacean quite like Barney in all their travels to that date. The fishing float enabled Sea Life staff and other experts to deduce how it was that Barney turned up where he did, and to conclude that he was, without doubt, one very lucky barnacle indeed.

Something must had dislodged him from his perch on the ocean floor. Perhaps it was an anchor dragging by or some large fish rooting among the rocks searching for something to eat. Whatever it was it almost spelled disaster, for, once uprooted, Barney was helpless to do anything other than float to the surface, where he was then unable to feed and where, as a result, he should very swiftly have perished.

Fate smiled kindly on Barney, however, and against odds of something like a trillion-to-one, along came the lost fishing float … the perfect liferaft. And instead of drifting further out into the wide seas, the float then washed up on Mull to be discovered by humans who happened to know enough about life along the seashore to realize that Barney was a shade out of the ordinary.

Staff at Oban fastened Barney's float to the bottom of one of their displays, and soon he was happily filtering away as if nothing had happened. Meanwhile the story of his miracle escape made a novel editorial item for many of Scotland's leading daily newspapers, a couple even sending photographers along to get pictures of a subject who, for once, needed no encouragement to keep perfectly still.

Barney seemed very much at home amidst a small colony of mussels and anemones, where, some months after his arrival, he performed the nearest thing that could be described as his star-turn, without a soul around to see it.

'I went to check on him one morning, and there were his old feelers lying on the bottom beside him,' said Terry Donovan. 'It's silly, of course, but I got the distinct impression he was looking a bit smug.'

Barney's new feathery feelers grew rapidly, and in the meantime a steady succession of admirers peered into his watery home as if willing him to do something spectacular. He never did, of course, though there was one gentleman who, after staring at Barney for what seemed an inordinately long time, finally departed with an expression of deep satisfaction, commenting to a staff member on his way out that Barney had slithered a good millimetre.

That Barney can be a real exhibitionist at times!

The Amazing Weymouth Squirrel Fish!

When David Mace selected the Dorset resort of Weymouth to host the second Sea Life Centre back in 1983, he was not unaware that the bountiful marine life in the nearby seas might occasionally yield the odd rarity.

Yet even he was surprised when, during the Centre's first full week of operation, local fisherman, Mick Reynolds, wandered in with what David recognized to be a type of Squirrel Fish. The basic characteristics of the species were familiar to him from his experiences with his own tropical fish collections as a youngster, and unlike those of any species commonly or even uncommonly found in British water, but which of the numerous different varieties this one was, he could not say. The new Centre was attracting far more attention than expected, so it is scarcely surprising that the curious four-inch-long orange fish was just popped into a convenient display tank and labelled simply 'Squirrel Fish', with little effort made during those first busy months to determine exactly which kind.

As the months and years rolled by, the Squirrel Fish grew, and from time to time one marine boffin or another would sift through the reference books to try and establish an accurate classification.

There were two significant obstacles to this process. First, most of the reference books themselves are woefully inadequate, which is again scarcely surprising considering the sheer numbers and diversity of subjects to be covered. Second, the numerous different races of Squirrel Fish differ in outward appearance only very marginally. As a result the Sea Life Centre's investigations could not narrow the field to fewer than half a dozen equally strong candidates.

So the years continued to roll by and the mystery persisted. All that could be said without fear of contradiction was that he was a Squirrel Fish, and a particularly handsome specimen. Indeed the arrival of the Centre's 10th anniversary saw the Squirrel Fish still happily patrolling his long display tank and now measuring over 25 centimetres long and about 10 centimetres high at his mid-section. He is a very pretty fish, with an almost golden sheen to some of his gleaming scales, and relatively large, dark and very alert eyes.

The mystery was finally solved by a man by the name of Alwyne Wheeler, a semi-retired ichthyologist (fish expert) from London's Natural History Museum. Alwyne had for many years been collecting details of unusual fish occurrences around the British Isles, and had lately become very interested in Weymouth's Squirrel Fish. The description supplied to him by Weymouth's own biological services manager, Mike Quarm, had been precise and detailed enough to raise an exciting suspicion, and now he wished to see photographic evidence before arranging a personal visit to make a first-hand identification. As luck would have it, one pin-sharp black-and-white print was available, and it was enough to bring Alwyne scurrying down to the Centre to confirm what he now already knew for certain … and I suspect also just to enable him to report later that he had 'seen it with his own two eyes!'

It turned out that the mystery fish which a surprised Mick Reynolds had plucked from a lobster pot near Portland Bill almost exactly ten years earlier was a species of Squirrel Fish normally confined to the Caribbean. And, although some are also found in the South Atlantic, the likelihood of a ten-centimetre fish swimming all the way to Portland Bill from either location seemed extremely remote.

This, ironically, excited Alwyne all the more, for it added weight to a theory he had developed to explain many of the stranger occurrences he had come across in his years of study, oddities like the Sea Bream from the Arabian Gulf caught in 1991 near the Eddystone Lighthouse just out from Plymouth, for example.

The Squirrel Fish was the first of its particular strain ever to be recorded in British waters, and, being a species rarely found in home aquarium collections, it was also unlikely to have been released deliberately into the sea.

Many scientists have pointed to phenomena such as this fish's appearance to support theories concerning global warming, but Alwyne had arrived at a different explanation; even stronger evidence in favour of his theory has lately been supplied by the mysterious appearance in

The Weymouth Squirrel Fish.

large numbers of a European freshwater species called the Ruffe in the North American great lakes.

'Clearly these fish could not have swum the Atlantic,' says Alwyne. 'I believe the only way they could have made the journey was in the ballast water taken in by a ship in freshwater dock in a European port, then ejected again when the ballast was released in port at the mouth of one of the rivers flowing from the lakes.'

Though almost impossible to prove, Alwyne's theory would also provide an explanation for the Squirrel Fish's appearance in the English Channel, which is far more plausible than any suggestion that it battled its way through the seas between there and the Caribbean or the South Atlantic.

For what it's worth, the Squirrel Fish's actual Latin classification is *Holocentrus Ascensionis*, the latter word taken from the name of Ascension Island, around the coast of which are found many other Squirrel Fish exactly like the one now swimming happily around its display at Weymouth Sea Life Park.

One thing is for certain, this story has provided Weymouth fisherman, Mick Reynolds, with a 'fisherman's tale' which is the envy of every other skipper in the harbour.

By Royal Appointment

At one time, probably not much more than a century ago, a truly majestic species of fish dwelled in coastal waters all around Europe and off the east side of North America. Every summer these fish would swim up most of the major European rivers to spawn, each female laying anything between 800,000 and 2½ million eggs. At the ripe old age of ten, this fish could measure one and a half metres long, but it would often continue to grow until it reached almost three metres, and weighed as much as 300 kilos.

With its long pointed snout, greeny-grey colouring and armour-plated body more akin to a reptile than a fish, the Common Sturgeon looked a creature from a pre-historic age, and today it is so scarce that many marine biologists believe it will soon have gone the way of the dinosaur.

There are still a few to be found in the Black Sea and its tributaries, but elsewhere they have either been fished almost out of existence or have vanished through no longer being able to reach their ancient spawning grounds, long since rendered inaccessible by the building of dams or other obstacles, or as a result of heavy pollution. In recent years attempts have been made to establish a sturgeon-farming operation in the South of France, but it is still too early to say whether this may help reverse the sturgeon's steady decline. In the meantime any appearance of a sturgeon around the coast of Britain is inevitably a once-in-a-lifetime event for those lucky enough to witness it.

When in early March 1992 a fisherman from Portland, Dorset, discovered a sturgeon tangled in his nets, research pointed to this being the first recorded capture of one off the Portland coast for more than eighty years. It certainly caused a bit of a stir when he delivered it to Weymouth Sea Life Park, where Robin James, Mike Quarm and their team settled it into a quarantine tank and attended to a number of minor cuts and abrasions it had picked up from the netting. Its ordeal had clearly caused it some stress, but Robin and Mike were hopeful that a period of rest and quiet would prove an adequate tonic.

Sea Life Park manager, Neil Biles, however, had another duty to perform, for a Royal statute laid down by Edward II, and never yet repealed, demands that any sturgeon caught in British waters be offered up for the Royal dining table. Of course, neither Neil nor any of his staff expected for one moment that the offer would be accepted, and had they been subsequently proved wrong I have no doubt that a mysterious and possibly 'treasonous' disappearance would have been effected. Fortunately the reply from Buckingham Palace was along the lines anticipated, and it showed that Her Majesty had considered the gesture to be far from trivial, or a waste of precious time.

Master of the Queen's Household, Rear Admiral Sir Paul Greening, wrote: 'The Queen does very much appreciate the

This old photograph of two French fishermen with a rare catch clearly illustrates the immense size Common Sturgeon may sometimes attain.

gesture in offering the fish to her. It is a tradition which she greatly values.'

And he added that Her Majesty was most interested and pleased that the fish was now being cared for at Weymouth Sea Life Park, and she wished for it to remain there.

Nothing would have delighted Robin and Mike more than to be able to place the sturgeon in Weymouth's spectacular British Sharks display, where it would have had ample swimming space and where it would undoubtedly have proved an immensely popular resident with the Park's thousands of visitors. From their studies of reports on earlier attempts by other European aquariums to display sturgeon, however, they learned that the species is notoriously nervy, and seldom adapts well to captive conditions. In spite of the great advertisement this fish could be for efforts to save its few surviving relatives from oblivion, nobody wished it to remain at the Sea Life Park unless it defied the previous pattern and proved itself to be both healthy and content in such circumstances. Whilst the sturgeon's wounds responded well to treatment, however, attempts to persuade it to feed proved less successful.

Happily, sturgeon can survive very long periods between meals, and the weight loss which this particular individual incurred was so gradual that Robin and Mike were half convinced it was actually helping itself to a few mouthfuls of shellfish whenever nobody was around. Such suspicions were not enough to satisfy either man, however, and so, once all signs of its external injuries had completely disappeared, arrangements were made to return the sturgeon to sea.

This happy event took place on Tuesday, August 11th, 1992, from a fishing boat a few miles out of Weymouth Quay, and the eagerness with which this rare beast took to the water finally convinced Robin and Mike that they had made the best decision. It was lowered into the waves by means of a cradle, and, once fully immersed, it simply gave one vigorous thrash of its tail and dived at speed towards the seabed. It measured only about 1.3 metres long, and was therefore probably no more than a couple of years old at most. I hope, as do Robin and Mike, that it is still out there somewhere feeding properly now, and that it survives to reach maturity at the age of eight or nine.

If it does, it may face a long and frustrating search to locate others of its own kind in order to breed … if indeed there are any others left by then to be found.

ABOVE Just a baby … this youngster is about one quarter of the length of the Common Sturgeon rescued by Weymouth Sea Life Park.
RIGHT Handful, the seal who was to become a keen traveller!

A Seal
Called 'Handful!'

The fact that so few of the creatures rescued and rehabilitated by Sea Life Centres are ever seen or heard of again is a source of both relief and frustration for the people who have cared for them.

On the one hand it suggests a resumption of a normal healthy life in the wild, but, on the other, it would be lovely to know for sure that they were coping well. One notable exception to this pattern was a Common Seal pup found abandoned on the beach at Holme, Norfolk, on July 1st, 1991. He was a male, weighing a skinny 8.8 kilos, but, other than being dehydrated and suffering a seemingly swollen right eye, he appeared in reasonable health.

With still 5 to 7 centimetres of umbilical chord clinging to him, he was clearly ony a few days old, but when staff from Hunstanton Sea Life Centre delivered him to the Centre's seal hospital, he responded well to their ministrations, eagerly gulping down the special baby food prepared for him and fed through a special tube.

By July 10th, he was beginning to show signs of a rather mischievous personality, and twice that day escaped from his cubicle and went on a tour of the hospital, visiting other recuperating infants. These exploits earned him the name Handful, and it was a name he was certainly destined to live up to.

By July 13th he was eating whole fish, and it was at this stage that he also began biting his feeders. He continued to go walkabout at every opportunity, and, since his attentions were not always friendly or helpful as far as other pups were concerned, staff built a makeshift barrier across his cubicle on July 20th, out of boxes, planks and a few other assorted items.

The following day they had to rebuild it again, and on the 23rd they were forced to start from scratch using much heavier obstacles. By July 31st Handful was happily feeding himself.

A comment on the Centre's record sheet at this time notes that:

'Handful seems to spend most of his time leaning upright against the front wall of his cubicle until someone walks past. He even sleeps in that position!'

On September 3rd, Handful was fitted with an identification tag bearing the number 25616, and the following day he was introduced to Hunstanton's outdoor seal pools. A month later his still swollen right eye appeared to be giving him problems. He seemed to be constantly squinting, but apart from the swelling there were no other visible signs of either injury or illness.

On October 11th Handful captured and devoured his first live fish, a sure sign that he was nearing readiness for a return to the wild; by now both his eyes seemed to be perfectly OK. He was finally released into The Wash on November 17th.

Aquarist Jeff Beck took a particular interest in Handful's release, because Handful had been the first abandoned seal pup he had ever been to collect, and as he watched the recovered pup swim off into The Wash he doubtless thought that was the last they would see or hear of him.

Towards the end of February the following year, however, a group of researchers from the Centre De Culture Scientifique at Brest in Northern France were patrolling the coast at the port of Trebuerden several miles east of Brest when they came across a seal lazing on the shoreline and were able to approach close enough to read his tag number ... sure enough, 25616.

In the middle of March, Handful was spotted again 88 miles further east at Granville, then again towards the end of April at St Quay-Portrieux, about 56 miles back in the other direction. Fearful for his safety, the French police captured him and delivered him to the Oceanopolis seal clinic in Brest. His right eye had now developed a small ulcer and he was a little underweight, but otherwise he was still fairly healthy.

Oceanopolis looked after him until July 2nd, 1992, when was released at a bay near Mont-St Michel, just to the south of Granville, where there is a small resident breeding colony of Common Seals.

Their company clearly was not good enough for Handful, however, who had now been fitted with a second small tag at the back of his head, so that he could be identified even at sea, when often the head is the only part of a seal which breaks the surface. Just sixteen days after his release Handful was seen in the River Garonne over 75 miles inland from the sea and about 288 miles due south of his release location.

Here he incurred the wrath of river fishermen, and for his own protection was again taken into custody, this time by the staff of Musée Oceanographique at La Rochelle. Nine days later he was transported overland to Brest and this time released in the bay at Brest.

Handful was not reported sighted again until nearly nine months later on March 5th, 1993, when he became a patient at the Norfolk Wildlife Hospital at Kings Lynn. He had been found on the beach at Felixstowe with a few small cuts and cloudy eyes.

Jeff Beck believes that Handful had become almost totally blind, and that this accounts for the fact that a beach walker at Felixstowe was able to quietly walk right up to him without startling Handful at all, until that same misguided walker reached out to stroke him. He needed hospital treatment for the damage to his hand! Handful, meanwhile weighed in at 42 kilos at Kings Lynn, which was 1.8 kilos heavier than his weight when last seen at Brest, so he was obviously managing to fend for himself in spite of his frequent visits to animal rescue centres of one kind or another.

The Wildlife Hospital fattened him up a bit more, and he was 57 kilos when released again on June 23rd.

Later that year Handful was spotted twice near salmon farms close to the Moray Firth in Scotland, and then soon after at Felixstowe again, when he was reported to be looking very fit and well.

'I can't wait to learn where he gets to next,' said Jeff Beck.

I could go on, and tell you about Twiggy, the Grey Seal who now resides at Gweek after seventeen years in the back yard of a Humberside pub; or about the rare Eagle Ray at Weymouth or the biggest Electric Ray in Britain which is living at Rhyl. But I have to stop somewhere; unless there is a demand for a second volume of *Saved from the Sea*. I must just tell you the most exciting news, however: following the successful reintroduction of Muddy and Spirit, Sea Life Centres are set to participate in a new monitoring network to respond to dolphin strandings, and may be setting up a National Rehabilitation Centre at Weymouth.